KAREN BROWN'S

California Country Inns & Itineraries

BOOKS IN KAREN BROWN'S COUNTRY INN SERIES

Austrian Country Inns & Castles

California Country Inns & Itineraries

English, Welsh & Scottish Country Inns

European Country Cuisine - Romantic Inns & Recipes

European Country Inns - Best on a Budget

French Country Bed & Breakfasts

French Country Inns & Chateaux

German Country Inns & Castles

Irish Country Inns

Italian Country Inns & Villas

Portuguese Country Inns & Pousadas

Scandinavian Country Inns & Manors

Spanish Country Inns & Paradors

Swiss Country Inns & Chalets

KAREN BROWN'S

California Country Inns & Itineraries

Written by

CLARE BROWN JUNE BROWN KAREN BROWN

Sketches by Barbara Tapp

Cover art by Christina Ladas

Karen Brown's Country Inn Series

WARNER BOOKS

Travel Press editors: Clare Brown, CTC, *June Brown,* CTC, *Karen Brown*
Iris Sandilands; technical support: William H. Brown, III

Illustrations: Barbara Tapp
Cover painting: Christina Ladas
Maps: Keith Cassell

This book is written in cooperation with:
Town and Country - Hillsdale Travel
16 East Third Avenue, San Mateo, California 94401

This Warner Books edition is published by arrangement with
Travel Press, San Mateo, California

Travel Press, P.O. Box 70, San Mateo, California 94401, U.S.A.

Warner Books, Inc., 666 Fifth Avenue, New York, NY 10103

A Warner Communications Company

Printed in the United States of America
First Printing: April 1989

Library of Congress Catalog Number: 88-40614

ISBN 0-446-39018-6 (pbk.) (U.S.A.)
0-446-39019-1 (pbk.) (Canada)

Travel Press San Mateo, California

Dedicated with Love and Hugs

to

Little Clare, Little Richard, Little Georgia

Contents

Foreword

For the past decade, every time we could escape for a few days, we were off to Europe combing the back roads for the most charming little inns. However, 1988 seemed a perfect year to stay home and write about our own back yard. The *official* reason for our switch to domestic travels was that, with the publication of our twelfth overseas guide, we had almost completed our European series. But the *real* reason for writing about our own state of California was that our production that year encompassed more than books - three babies joined our troops. We are thankful to our little ones for the excuse to savor the grandeur of California - we really never dreamed of the wonders awaiting us. Every week it was off into the countryside, sightseeing and ferreting out special places to stay. Each moment was an adventure, from clambering aboard a little boat to inspect a lighthouse tucked on its own tiny island to driving to the northernmost reaches of California to see an old stagecoach stop nestled high in the mountains. We have maintained the same standards as in our European guides: every inn included has been personally inspected and chosen for its special charm, every itinerary has been "run" to be sure it really works. It was a year of great fun exploring California and, as always, we love sharing our discoveries with you.

Introduction

California is a fascinating state: a treasure chest just waiting to be opened, filled with gorgeous scenery, exciting things to do and wonderful places to stay. There is almost too much - it can be confusing to decide the most important sights to see and the most special inns to choose. This book is written to help you through the maze: we have done your homework for you.

To find the most special places to stay, letters were written to over seven hundred inns. After receiving their replies and studying the merits of each, those that did not seem to reflect the charm we were seeking were rejected. Then we visited those places that looked most promising - more than five hundred inns were seen, but less than one out of every four was selected. We wish more travellers were aware how misleading many guide books are when recommending places to stay: the majority of inn books on the market are not very selective - to be included the owners have to pay. The payment can take various forms: sometimes the innkeeper pays outright for inclusion and even writes his own recommendation; another gimmick is that the owner must pay for an ad or color photographs; at other times, the books are listings of inns which pay to belong to an affiliation. This is not to say that these other guides are without merit. But it does mean that they include many inns which we rejected and also leave out some of the very best inns whose attributes are so outstanding that they do not need to pay for advertising. No hotel has ever paid to be included in any of our travel books, and this one is no exception. However, quite frankly, our guides are very prejudiced: the inns selected to be included are those we personally liked.

The five itineraries in this guide spider-web across the state, so you can choose one that includes the area you had your heart set upon visiting. Each routing can easily be tailored to meet your own specific needs by leaving out some of the overnight stops if time is limited, or linking several itineraries together if you wish to enjoy a longer vacation.

ABOUT THE ITINERARIES

Below is some general information that we hope answers questions you may have about the itineraries and your travel planning.

CAR RENTAL: The itineraries are designed for travel by automobile. If you are staying in San Francisco before heading into the countryside, you do not need to pick up your rental car until the day you leave since the public transportation system is so convenient and this is a town made for walking. However if your vacation begins in Los Angeles you will need a car to get from place to place and should pick it up on arrival at the airport.

DRIVING TIMES: California is a large state, approximately 1,000 miles from tip to toe. If you stay on the expressways you can quickly cover large areas of territory, but if you choose to savor the beauty of the coast along California's sensational highway 1 or dip into the countryside along the scenic backroads, plan on travelling about 30 miles in an hour and remember to allow extra time for stopping to enjoy countryside vistas. Also, keep in mind that inclement weather such as heavy fog on the coast or in the central valley can impede your progress.

MAPS: Each itinerary has a map outlining the suggested routing and marking sightseeing and overnight stops. Alternate places to stay are also marked. The maps are an artist's renderings and do not show every road and highway - you need to supplement them with detailed commercial maps. Another tip: before your trip secure street maps of larger cities and pinpoint the exact location of your hotels.

WEATHER: At the end of each itinerary a brief note is given on what you can expect to encounter weatherwise along the way. In California a whole new clime emerges by travelling just a short distance. The idea that the entire state is sunny and warm year round can all too quickly be dispelled when the summer fog rolls into San Francisco or 3 feet of winter snow falls in the High Sierras.

ABOUT INN TRAVEL

A wide range of inns is included in this guide: some are great bargains - others very costly; some are in cities - others in remote locations; some are quite sophisticated - others extremely simple; some are decorated with opulent antiques - others with furniture from grandma's attic; some are large hotels - others have only a few rooms. The common denominator is that each place has some special quality that makes it appealing. To help you appreciate and understand what to expect when travelling the "Inn Way", the following pointers are given.

AIR CONDITIONING: Many parts of California are hot during the summer months. Most of the inns do not have air conditioning, so be sure to inquire in advance if you have a problem with the heat.

BATHROOMS: Many inns do not have a private bathroom for each guest room. Be sure to discuss the bathroom situation when making a reservation. The number of bedrooms and bathrooms are listed at the bottom of each hotel description.

BREAKFAST: Breakfast can range from a gourmet feast to a simple roll and a cup of coffee to nothing at all. If breakfast is NOT included in the room rate we say so.

CANCELLATION POLICIES: Inns are usually more stringent than chain hotels in their cancellation policies: be sure to discuss this when you make a reservation.

CHARM: It is very important that an inn has charm - ideally an inn should be a historic building, beautifully decorated, lovingly managed and in a wonderful location. Few inns meet every criterion, but all our selections have some particular ambiance that makes them special and are situated in enjoyable surroundings - we have had to reject several lovely inns because of a poor location. Many are in historic buildings, but you must remember that California is a relatively new state, so anything over 50 years in age is considered old - few inns date back further than the mid-19th century and many are new or reproduction-old buildings.

CHECK-IN: Inns are usually very specific about check-in time - generally between 3:00PM and 6:00PM. Let the inn know if you are going to arrive late and the innkeeper will make special arrangements for you, such as leaving you a door key under a potted plant along with a note on how to find your room.

CHILDREN: Most places in this guide do not welcome children. Under each listing we have indicated the general policy, but these are only guidelines. Many places will accept children if they have the proper room available, if the children are teenagers, if other families are going to be in residence or if it is a slow period.

CREDIT CARDS: Whether or not an establishment accepts credit cards is indicated at the bottom of each description - AX (American Express), MC (Master Card), VS (Visa), all major, or none accepted. Even if an inn does not accept plastic payment it will often take your credit card number as a guarantee of arrival.

FRIENDLINESS: The warmth of reception is extremely important in making a stay at an inn a happy experience, so we paid particular attention to the friendliness of the innkeepers.

PROFESSIONALISM: All the inns we selected are run by professional innkeepers. There are many homes that rent out extra bedrooms to paying guests but this was not what we were looking for and they are not included in our guide. We have recommended only inns that have privacy for the guests and where you do not have to climb over little Freddie's tricycle to reach the bathroom.

RESERVATIONS: The best way to make a reservation is to just pick up your phone and call. In the majority of inns each bedroom has its own personality, so it is very helpful to discuss the various types of accommodation available. When planning your trip be aware that the majority of inns in this guide require a two night stay on weekends and during holiday periods.

ROOM RATES: It seems that many inns play musical rates, having high season, low season, midweek, weekend and holiday rates. We have quoted the 1989 high season range of rates for two people occupying a bedroom: singles usually receive a very small discount. We have not discussed "special" rooms such as those that can accommodate three people travelling together and we have not included luxurious suites in our rates - discuss with the innkeeper what rooms are available and make your choice. Taxes are not included in our room rates; breakfast is included. Of course, several hotels are exceptions to our guidelines and whenever this is the case we mention it.

SIZE: Small inns are usually our favorites, but size alone did not dictate whether or not a hostelry was chosen. Most are small (one has only two guest rooms), but because California offers some splendid larger establishments of great character and charm a few of these are also included.

SMOKING: Nearly all the inns forbid smoking in the bedrooms. Some allow no smoking at all. Ask about smoking policies if this is important to you - best to be forewarned rather than frustrated.

SOCIALIZING: Inns usually offer a conviviality rarely found in a "standard" hotel. The gamut runs all the way from playing "cozy family" around the kitchen table to sharing a sophisticated, coolly elegant cocktail hour in the parlor. Breakfast may be a formal meal served at a set hour when the guests gather around the dining room table, or it may be a buffet-style meal served over several hours where guests make themselves a plate of food and then have the option of either sitting down to eat alone or joining other guests at a larger table. Then again, some inns will bring a breakfast tray to your room. Another social opportunity is the cocktail hour: in the evening some establishments provide hors d'oeuvres and wine over a long period of time and guests meander in and out mixing or not mixing with other guests as they choose. Sometimes there are more formal cocktail parties, often with the innkeeper presiding. What you need to do is choose the inn that seems to offer the degree of togetherness that you desire.

WHEN YOU COME HOME

Our greatest resource is you, our readers. Some of our favorite inns and most spectacular sights are those you have shared with us. Things change from the way we observed them and we rely on you to keep us abreast of these changes. Thank you so much for taking the time to contact us with your impressions - they have been invaluable. As this book goes to press, we have done our best to provide you with what we think are the most outstanding places to stay. We have tried to be honest in our appraisal of each inn and as accurate as possible. On the other hand, we have most certainly left out some gems unknown to us. When you come home from your holiday, please share your experiences with us. *We are also constantly updating our guide books to Europe, so if you have any favorite inns in Austria, England, France, Germany, Ireland, Italy, Portugal, Scandinavia, Scotland, Spain, Switzerland or Wales we would love to hear about them.*

San Francisco to Los Angeles via the Coast

San Francisco
San Jose
Felton
SANTA CRUZ
Monterey
San Juan Bautista
Pacific Grove
17 Mile Drive
CARMEL
Julia Pfeiffer Burns State Park
Hearst Castle
CAMBRIA
Morro Bay
San Luis Obispo
Pismo Beach
Guadalupe
Mission La Purisma
Solvang
SANTA BARBARA
Los Angeles

Overnight Stops
★ Alternate Places to Stay
● Points of Reference

San Francisco to Los Angeles via the Coast

Cable Car - San Francisco

You can drive between San Francisco and Los Angeles in a day or fly in an hour. But rather than rushing down the freeway or hopping aboard an airplane, drive leisurely along the coast between these two metropolises and enjoy the solitude of redwood forests, the quaintness of Carmel, the charm of Santa Barbara, the splendor of the Big Sur Coast, the opulence of William Randolph Hearst's hilltop castle, and the fun of experiencing a bit of Denmark in Solvang. Also intertwined in this itinerary are stops to appreciate a piece of California's colorful heritage - her Spanish missions. This routing roughly follows the footsteps of the Spanish padres who, in the 1700s, built a string of missions (about a day's journey apart) along the coast of California from the Mexican border to just north of San Francisco. Today many of these beautiful adobe churches and their surrounding settlements have been reconstructed and are open as museums, capturing a glimpse of life as it was lived by the Spaniards and the Indians in the early days of colonization.

When you ask travellers around the world, "What is your favorite city?" many times the answer is "San Francisco". And it is no wonder. SAN FRANCISCO really is very special, a magical town of unsurpassed beauty - spectacular when glistening in the sunlight, equally enchanting when wrapped in fog. But the beauty is more than skin deep: San Francisco offers a wealth of sightseeing, fabulous restaurants, splendid shopping, and a refreshing climate.

There are many large, super-deluxe hotels in San Francisco plus a marvelous selection of small, intimate inns. Study our various recommendations to see what most fits your personality and pocketbook. Be advised that hotel space is frequently very tight, so make reservations as far in advance as possible.

A good way to orient yourself with San Francisco is to take a half-day city sight-seeing tour (brochures on these tours should be available at your hotel) and then return to the destinations that most catch your fancy. If you like to study before you arrive, there are entire guide books devoted to San Francisco and the Visitors' Bureau will send you an information packet on what to see and do in the city (San Francisco Visitors' Bureau, P.O. Box 6977, San Francisco, CA 94101, telephone (415) 391-2000.) To keep you on the right track here are some of our favorite sights:

ALCATRAZ: A visit to the prison island in the middle of San Francisco Bay is a fascinating excursion. This lonely, concrete, fortress-like structure seemed escape-proof until (so the story goes) a prisoner dug his way out with a spoon. The tour involves lots of walking, so be sure to wear sturdy, comfortable shoes and don't forget your wooly sweater because it is cold on this windswept rocky island. This excursion is very popular. For further information call (415) 546-2800.

CABLE CARS: You cannot leave San Francisco without riding one of the colorful little trolleys which make their way up and down the breathtakingly steep city hills. Rather than taking a cab or a bus, plan your sightseeing around hopping on and off cable cars. For a behind-the-scenes look at this charmingly antiquated transit system visit the Cable Car Museum at the corner of Washington and Mason Streets. Here you can view the huge cables which pull the cars from below the streets and a historical display which includes the first cable car.

CALIFORNIA PALACE OF THE LEGION OF HONOR: If you have time for only one museum, this is it. The art and the setting are spectacular. Set in parklike grounds on a bluff overlooking the ocean, the views are magnificent. The front of the museum is a courtyard where Rodin sculptures are displayed. Within, 18th- and 19th-century French artists are featured, but, in addition to the permanent art collection, there is always some interesting travelling exhibit to see. The museum is located on Legion of Honor Drive in Lincoln Park. For further information call (415) 750-3600.

CHINATOWN: Just a few short blocks from Union Square you enter beneath the dragon arch (at the corner of Bush Street and Grant Avenue) into another world: street signs in Chinese characters, tiny grocery stores displaying Chinese vegetables and groceries, apothecary shops selling unusual remedies, spicy aromas drifting from colorful restaurants, older women bustling about in traditional dress, the hum around you of unfamiliar phrases. Of course the streets are jammed with tourists and there are a lot of rather tacky souvenir shops. Don't limit your exploration of Chinatown to the main thoroughfare of Grant Avenue: poke down the intriguing little alleys and side streets. You can plan a visit to 56 Ross Alley to visit the Golden Gate Fortune Cookie Factory. Down another alley, at 17 Adler Place, you find the Chinese Historical Society of America - a small fascinating museum, telling the story of the Chinese immigration.

COIT TOWER: Coit Tower, located at the top of Telegraph Hill, is a relic of old San Francisco and fun to visit ... not only because the view is great, but because its story is so *very San Francisco.* The money to construct the watch tower, which resembles the nozzle on a firehose, was willed to the city by the wealthy Lillie Hitchcock Coit, a volunteer fireman (or should we say firewoman) who dearly loved to rush to every blaze wearing her diamond-encrusted fire badge. A mural on the ground floor provides a vivid depiction of early California life.

ESPRIT: Anyone interested in needlework should make a special effort to visit the Esprit Corporate Offices located about a 15-minute drive south of the center of town. Here you find a splendid collection of Amish quilts magnificently displayed. You can come any weekday from 10:00AM to 4:00PM. Admission is $4.00 per person and a self guided tour leads you through 3 floors of fantastic quilts. Note: if you have a young daughter, by all means visit the Esprit clothing outlet just a few blocks away at the corner of 16th and Illinois Streets. Esprit is located at 900 Minnesota Street. For further information call (415) 648-6900.

FISHERMAN'S WHARF: Fisherman's Wharf has long been a favorite with tourists. However, it is difficult to find even the small heart of Fisherman's Wharf behind all the plastic trinket-filled souvenir shops and tacky tourist arcades. But look carefully, and sure enough you will see the colorful fishing boats bobbing about in the water at the waterfront between Jones and Taylor streets. Nearby, Fish Alley, a small pier extending out into the harbor, gives you a good view of the fishing fleet and the aroma of fresh fish mingling with the salty air. Snug on Fish Alley is the excellent Ascona fish restaurant. At Pier 43 you find the three-masted Scottish merchant ship, the Balclutha, which is open as a museum. Pier 39 is lined with newly constructed New England-style shops; nothing authentic, but a popular shopping and restaurant arcade (most of the shops are ones you will see at any tourist arcade in the United States).

FORT POINT: Nestled at the base of the Golden Gate Bridge's south pier, Fort Point, built in 1861 as one of the west coast's principal points of defense, provides both a fascinating insight into military life during that period and a most unusual view of the famous bridge. For more information call (415) 556-1693.

GHIRARDELLI SQUARE: A few blocks from Fisherman's Wharf, in a wonderful old brick building which used to house the Ghirardelli Chocolate Factory, you will find one of San Francisco's most appealing places for browsing. The complex consumes one full square block which climbs steeply up a hillside, adding much variety to the design of the interior. Tucked within you will find a wealth of things to buy in the more than 80 little shops, then, when you get hungry, there are more than a dozen excellent restaurants from which to choose. Flower gardens and free entertainment add to the fun of shopping.

GOLDEN GATE PARK: Unless you are an enthusiastic jogger, you will need to take a bus or taxi to Golden Gate Park, but don't miss it. The park encompasses over 1000 acres, so large you really cannot hope to see it all, but many attractions are located within a manageable proximity. So, if you take a cab, ask to be let out at one, and you can walk to the others. Visit the Japanese Tea Garden, the De Young Museum, the Steinhart Aquarium and the Planetarium in the Academy of Sciences. If you have a car, explore the entire park, a treasure of lakes, gardens and green lawns.

LOMBARD STREET: Lombard Street is an ordinary road - except for one lone block between Hyde and Leavenworth where the brick-paved street goes crazy and makes a series of hairpin turns as it twists downwards. Pretty houses border each side of the street, and banks of hydrangeas add to the happy scene. Start at the top and go down what must be the crookedest street in the world: it is lots of fun.

MISSION SAN FRANCISCO DE ASIS: This mission is frequently referred to as the Mission Dolores; but, no matter what you call it, if you are interested in Californian missions you will find a visit here worthwhile. It was on this spot that

San Francisco was really born when Father Francisco Palou founded his mission here in 1776. At one time this was a large complex of warehouses, workshops, granaries, a tannery, soap shop, corrals, Indian dwellings and even an aqueduct. Today, all that is left is the chapel and next to it the garden where gravestones attest to the fragility of life. Although small, the chapel is beautiful in its simplicity with 4-foot-thick adobe walls and massive redwood timbers.

NATIONAL MARITIME MUSEUM: This ship-shaped building at the foot of Polk Street in Aquatic Park has displays on the history of water transportation from the 1800s to the present, including some marvelous photos of old San Francisco and exquisite exhibits of scrimshaw. Fascinating for the landlubber as well as the old or young sea salt. Closed on Mondays and Tuesdays.

TIBURON: A really fun excursion is to take the ferry from Pier 1 in San Francisco to Tiburon, a small town on a tiny peninsula across the bay. Tiburon is loaded with charm - appealing little shops, intriguing small art galleries and wonderful restaurants tucked into the little New England-style village. As a bonus, en route you enjoy wonderful vistas of San Francisco. For further information call (415) 546-2815.

UNION SQUARE: In the center of the city is Union Square, hallmarked by a small park around which tower deluxe hotels and fancy department stores. Do not tarry too long at the "biggies" because the really fun browsing can be found by wandering a block or so away where you will discover an irresistible assortment of specialty stores. Some of our favorites are: FAO Schwartz, which caters to the child in all of us, 180 Post Street; Gumps, elegant gifts, 250 Post Street; Jeffrey Davies, beautiful silk flower arrangements and antiques, 575 Sutter Street; La Ville du Soleil, fun, whimsical shop with cookware, gifts and antiques, 444 Post Street; Laura Ashley, country-English clothing and fabrics, 563 Sutter; Pierre Deux, French fabrics and gifts, 532 Sutter; Thomas Brothers Maps, a wonderful assortment of maps, 550 Jackson Street; Williams-Sonoma, gourmet cookware, 576 Sutter Street.

UNION STREET: Union Street, lined with lovely restored Victorian houses, is a bit away from the center of town, but offers a wonderful variety of quaint gift shops, elegant boutiques, beautiful antique stores, small art galleries and excellent restaurants. As you browse, watch for intriguing little shops hidden down tiny brick-paved lanes.

DESTINATION I — SANTA CRUZ

There is no need to rush your departure today as your destination for tonight lies just two hours' drive from San Francisco. Leave the city heading south on highway 280 (19th Avenue leads directly onto this freeway). Soon San Francisco and her suburbs melt into countryside as the road traces the Crystal Springs Reservoir, a series of lakes that follow the San Andreas earthquake fault. With the wooded coastal hills as a backdrop, highway 280 is considered one of California's most beautiful freeways and quickly speeds you down the San Francisco peninsula. Continue on highway 280 through the suburbs of San Jose until you come to highway 17 which you take heading west toward Santa Cruz. Highway 17 bypasses the attractive town of Los Gatos and then climbs into the forested coastal hills. Soon after reaching the summit of the pass, take the second Scotts Valley exit, signposted Glen Canyon - Mt Herman Road, and follow signs for FELTON and BIG BASIN.

A 10-minute drive brings you to Graham Hill Road where you turn left for the short drive to ROARING CAMP RAILROAD, a fun means of seeing and learning about a coastal redwood forest. After parking your car, walk past the duck pond and across the little covered bridge into a cluster of buildings which includes the depot where you purchase your train tickets. The train leaves several times a day - call to verify the departure times for the date you will be travelling on (408) 335-4400. Reservations cannot be made in advance, but mid-week and off season you should not have a problem getting on the first train out. Just before time of departure, an old-fashioned steam engine chugs up to the depot and fills its tank with water while the passengers climb into mustard yellow open cars. Soon the conductor hoots the horn, then off the train chugs up into the trees along narrow gauge tracks built to carry lumber out of the forest. Along the way, the conductor tells stories of the "old days" as the train circles up through the trees, making a brief stop at the "cathedral", a beautiful ring of redwoods which form a natural outdoor church, before heading back into town. A suggestion would be to plan to eat lunch at Roaring Camp: that way, should you arrive early, you can dine while waiting. (Hamburgers and hot dogs can be purchased at a little red caboose in the village center.) Another option would be to picnic along the way. A stop is made en route at a lovely redwood glen where passengers can get off and wait for the next train.

After the train ride, drive out of the parking lot and turn right on Graham Hill Road. SANTA CRUZ is well-signposted, only about a 15-minute drive west of Roaring Camp. Years ago this busy seaside town, with its bustling boardwalk and amusement park bordering a broad stretch of white sand beach, was a popular day-trip for workers in San Francisco. In recent years the rides and attractions have received a facelift, making it a pleasure to visit. The rides include a heart-stopping wooden Big Dipper and a wonderful old-fashioned carousel. An effort is being made to make the adjacent fishing pier attractive with restaurants and shops.

A short drive from the center of town, terraced down a small hillside and bordering a stream, is the delightful BABBLING BROOK INN. Several exquisitely decorated country-style bedrooms are in the main lodge while the remainder are in small buildings along the creek. Most rooms have private balconies that overlook meandering pathways and a profusion of flowers that border the chattering little brook.

The Babbling Brook Inn
Santa Cruz

DESTINATION II CARMEL

Today's first sightseeing destination is one of California's loveliest missions, SAN JUAN BAUTISTA, which lies south and inland from Santa Cruz. Leave town on highway 1 and drive south for about 20 miles until you come to highway 129 where you head east. Continue on the 129 for approximately 16 miles through small farms and rolling hills to San Juan Bautista. An area of the town has been restored to the way it was 150 years ago with the mission as its focus. Facing the square is the restored Plaza Hotel, now a museum where tickets are sold to visit the points of interest in the park. The focal point of the sightseeing is, of course, the mission, but do not end your touring there. Directly across from the mission is a most interesting house, nicely restored and furnished as it must have looked many years ago. Adjacent to this is a blacksmith shop and stables where there is a colorful display of old coaches. Next door to the Plaza Hotel is another home now open as a museum with period furnishings. After seeing the mission complex, walk into the town of San Juan Bautista, which still maintains its 19th-century, small town ambiance.

When leaving San Juan Bautista, follow highway 156 west for a couple of miles until it merges with the 101 going south to the Monterey Peninsula. As you pass through PRUNEDALE, begin to watch for signs indicating a sharp right-hand turn on the 156 west to the Monterey Peninsula.

Along the way, fields of artichokes come into view as you near CASTROVILLE, the artichoke capital of the world. When you begin to smell the sea air, stay in the left lane following signs for highway 1 south to the Monterey Peninsula. As you approach Monterey, dunes lining the sweep of the bay come into view. Watch carefully and take the first exit onto Del Monte Avenue which you follow for about a mile, staying in the right-hand lane so you can park along the marina.

The main sightseeing attractions in MONTEREY are in two areas: the first, Old Town and Fisherman's Wharf; the second (about a mile away), Cannery Row and Monterey Bay Aquarium.

The parking area at the marina puts you within walking distance of OLD TOWN where a 3-mile walking tour links the restored buildings of early Monterey. You won't have time to take the complete path - just confine your wanderings to the adobes nearest the marina and then go on to visit the nearby FISHERMAN'S WHARF, a quaint wooden fishing pier lined with shops and restaurants. At the end of the pier huge sea lions vie for the fish that tourists buy in little packets to feed to them.

From the Marina it is a short, well-marked drive to CANNERY ROW and the Aquarium. Cannery Row, once the center of this area's thriving sardine industry (the fish are long gone) and brought vividly to life by John Steinbeck in his novels featuring Doc and the boys, is now filled with touristy shops, but the adjacent

MONTEREY BAY AQUARIUM is outstanding and should not be missed (for information call (408) 375-3333). The centerpieces of the Aquarium are the huge glass tanks that showcase the underwater world of the local offshore marine life: one tank is populated by huge sharks and colorful schools of fish while another contains a mature kelp forest crowded with fish.

Monterey is all hustle and bustle (especially in summer) and it is quite a relief to continue to the neighboring, much quieter town of PACIFIC GROVE, just a few miles away. To reach Pacific Grove, follow the road in front of the Aquarium and make a right turn onto Ocean View Boulevard, a lovely drive lined on one side with gracious Victorian homes and splendid views of the sea on the other. Besides being an affluent residential community, Pacific Grove is famous for the Monarch butterflies which return each October and cluster in the grove of trees next to Butterfly Grove Inn on Lighthouse Avenue. The butterflies return faithfully every year, just as the swallows return to San Juan Capistrano.

Carmel lies just a few miles beyond Pacific Grove and there is no more perfect way to arrive than along the famous 17-Mile Drive that meanders around the Monterey Peninsula coastline between the two towns. The route is easy to find as the road which leads to the "drive" intersects Lighthouse Avenue and is appropriately called 17-Mile Drive.

THE 17-MILE DRIVE loops through an exclusive residential area of multi-million-dollar estates and gorgeous golf courses. Because the land is private, $5 per car is levied at the entrance gate. When you pay the toll, you receive a map indicating points of interest along the way. The drive traces the low-lying shore, passes rocky coves where kelp beds are home to sea lions, sea otters, cormorants and gulls (remember to bring your binoculars) and meanders through woodlands where Monterey pines gnarled by the wind stand sentinel on lonely headlands. Along the drive is the famous Pebble Beach Golf Course, site of the National Pro-Am Golf Championship every January.

As you exit through the southern gate of the 17-Mile Drive, Carmel is well signposted. Follow Ocean Boulevard into the heart of the town and turn left on Junipero to the COBBLESTONE INN. An appealing cobblestone facade, paved parking courtyard, trees and colorful flowers have transformed what was once a very ordinary motel into a delightful country inn, decorated in a cute country decor with teddy bears as accent pieces. The whimsical theme of teddy bears as accents is continued in the cheerful lounge and dining room. Each of the bedrooms is prettily decorated in a country motif and has the added bonus of a fireplace.

Cobblestone Inn
Carmel

CARMEL is a most appealing town, filled with Hansel and Gretel-style cottages nestled under pines and surrounded by flower-filled gardens. Tourists throng the streets lined with lovely boutiques, pretty gift stores, appetizing sweet shops, beckoning bakeries and a wonderful selection of cozy restaurants.

Although Carmel is oozing with charm, it is the bay which makes it so special. The main street in town slopes gently down the hill, ending at a gorgeous white sand beach backed by large, windswept sand dunes.

Just south of town is the exquisite MISSION CARMEL, established in 1770 by Father Junipero Serra. Beautifully restored and fronted by a delightful garden, the mission was Father Serra's headquarters and it is from here that the stalwart little priest set out to expand the chain of missions. A small museum shows the simple cell in which Father Serra slept on a hard wooden bed. The church itself, with its Moorish tower, star-shaped window and profusion of surrounding flowers, has a most romantic appearance.

Located just south of Carmel on highway 1 is another place you must not miss, POINT LOBOS STATE RESERVE, one of the loveliest spots on the California coast. A small admission fee gives you day use of the park. Drive through the woods to the headlands where rocky coves are home to sea lions and sea otters. Walking trails are well marked and the times of guided nature walks are posted at the entrance gate.

DESTINATION III — CAMBRIA

Believe everything you ever read about the beauties of the BIG SUR coastline: it is truly sensational. However, hope for clear weather, because on foggy or rainy days an endless picture of stunning seascapes becomes a tortuous drive around precipitous cliff roads. (If the weather is inclement you may wish to take the inland route to Cambria by following the picturesque Carmel Valley road east to Highway 101 where you then head south. When you come to highway 46, turn west. The road intersects with the coastal highway 1 just south of Cambria.)

As you drive south on highway 1, you know you are approaching Big Sur when you see the road sign "Hill Curves 63 miles" which is exactly what the road does as it clings precipitously to the edge of the cliff along many portions of today's drive.

While the road is quite narrow, there are plenty of turnouts that offer photographic opportunities.

The highway passes over the much photographed long, concrete span of Bixby Creek bridge. A few miles later the rocky volcanic outcrop topped by the Point Sur Lighthouse appears. About 40 miles south of Carmel you come to PFEIFFER BIG SUR STATE PARK with its camping facilities and many miles of hiking trails amongst coastal redwood groves.

If you choose only one place to stop along the Big Sur drive, make it NEPENTHE (about 3 miles south of the entrance to Pfeiffer Big Sur State Park). Nepenthe is a casual restaurant, with a sixties-style decor, perched on a cliff high above the ocean offering unsurpassed views (on a bright day) of the coast to the south. Even if you are not in the mood for a substantial meal you can enjoy coffee and dessert on the lower terrace at the Cafe Amorpha. Interestingly, the heart of the complex is a cottage that Orson Welles bought for his then wife Rita Hayworth.

Another stop along the way where you can gain a closer view of this magnificent coastline is at the JULIA PFEIFFER BURNS STATE PARK. The parking area is to the left of the road. Leave your car and take the short walk leading under the highway and round the face of the cliff which overlooks a superb small cove with emerald green water and a white sand beach. From the rocky bluff a waterfall drops directly into the ocean and the restless sea beats against a craggy point.

After you pass the Ragged Point Inn, the bends become less frequent, and, as the cliffs give way to the coastal plain, the driving becomes far less arduous. After the road begins to flatten out, watch for HEARST CASTLE shimmering in the heat haze high on a hill to your left. In 1919 William Randolph Hearst commissioned California's famous architect Julia Morgan to design a simple vacation home atop a hill on his estate overlooking the California coastline. Twenty-eight years and $10,000,000 later his 100-room retreat, La Cuesta Encantada (the enchanted hill) was complete. Now more commonly known as Hearst Castle, the enchanted hill continues to delight the millions of visitors who marvel at the skill in which priceless art, valuable furniture, historic tapestries, remains of European castles, Greek temples, carved ceilings and Persian rugs were incorporated into this showpiece home. And the grandeur does not stop at the castle complex - the gardens required the planting of over 100,000 trees and 70 species of animals roamed in 2,000 fenced acres of grounds (almost everything from apes to yaks). The whole place certainly stands as testament to William Randolph Hearst's quotation "Pleasure is worth what you can afford to pay for it." The whole place is undeniably grandiose, but even the most sceptical of persons has to admit that it has a certain magic.

Next to Disneyland, Hearst Castle is the most popular visitor attraction in California and, because the number of visitors allowed on the hill during any one day is limited, it is essential that you make reservations in advance. Tours begin at 8:20AM daily (closed Thanksgiving, Christmas and New Year's Day) and the last tour starts at 3:00PM (later in summer). Because there is so much to see, four very different tours are offered. Each tour lasts about 1 hour and 45 minutes. Each tour costs $10.00 (1989) per person and reservations can be prepaid on a credit card by calling from California (1-800) 444-7275, or from outside California (619) 452-1950. Tours are placed on sale eight weeks in advance. For the purposes of this itinerary, it is recommended that you make reservations for the last tour of the day so that you can savor the beauty of Big Sur en route.

Plan on arriving at the Visitors' Center at the foot of the hill at least half an hour before your scheduled departure, as the tours depart with clockwork-like precision and do not wait for stragglers. If you arrive early, you can browse through the small museum located next to the departure depot where groups assemble by number for their turn to be taken up the hill by bus.

Tour 1, the overview of the castle, is the one recommended for first-time visitors. You walk through the gardens to the main house, La Casa Grande, to tour the rooms on the lower level. The sheer size and elaborate decor of the assembly room where Hearst gathered with his guests before dinner sets the opulent mood of this elegant establishment. In the adjoining refectory Hearst and his guests dined in a re-created medieval banquet hall - the bottles of Hearst's favorite ketchup on the table seemed rather out of place. In the theater a short home movie of Hearst and some of his celebrity friends gives you an idea of life at the castle during the 1930s. A feeling for the opulence of the guest accommodation is given as you tour the bedrooms of the guest house Casa del Sol. The indoor Roman Pool has over half a million Italian mosaic tiles, vast amounts of gold leaf and took over five years to complete.

Tour 2 views suites of bedrooms, the kitchen and the swimming pools. Tour 3 shows you the guest wing of the castle, a guest house and the pools. Tour 4 is offered only in summer, does not go into the main house and focuses on the gardens.

From the Hearst-San Simeon State Historical Monument it is just an 8-mile drive south to your recommended overnight stop, THE J. PATRICK HOUSE in Cambria. CAMBRIA was once a whaling station and a dairy town that shipped butter and cheese to San Francisco. Now the main town lies away from the coast and encompasses two streets of art galleries, gift shops, antique stores and restaurants. To find The J. Patrick House, take the first Cambria exit from highway 1, follow Main Street through town to East Cambria Village where you turn right on Burton. Follow Burton as it leads past more shops and restaurants before making a turn to the left and weaving up the hill. Almost at the top of the incline, turn right: on your left is The J. Patrick House. At first glance the home seems to be an old, early-American log cabin. But looks can be deceiving - the J. Patrick House is actually of new construction, cleverly incorporating bits and pieces of authentically old cabins. Some of the bedrooms are in the main house, others (all with a fireplace) are located in a pretty two-story house facing the back garden.

The J. Patrick House
Cambria

DESTINATION IV — SANTA BARBARA

The most dramatic part of the coast lies behind you, but the fun of driving along miles of beach, exploring one of California's most beautiful missions, seeing a "reproduction" Danish village and visiting the elegant resort of Santa Barbara await.

Leave Cambria on highway 1 going south. The road leaves the coast and travels through low-lying hills to SAN LUIS OBISPO, merging with the 101 travelling south. If you want to visit every mission en route, when you reach San Luis Obispo take the Broad Street exit and follow directions to the mission which lies at the heart of this busy town. (Although it is an interesting mission, the setting does not compare in beauty with others included in this itinerary.)

About 10 miles south of San Luis Obispo the 1/101 returns to the coast at Pismo

Beach where you take the exit for highway 1 and PISMO BEACH, a 12-mile arc of white sand beach backed in part by dunes. This is the home of the famous Pismo clam which has unfortunately in recent years become rather scarce. As you travel south on highway 1, views of the beach are blocked by apartments, motels and unattractive housing developments, but do not despair: 2 miles after leaving the freeway, turn right into PISMO BEACH STATE PARK. After paying the entrance fee, pass quickly over the soft sand. Once your tires hit the well-packed, damp sand, your way feels more secure as you drive along the beach, paralleling the crashing waves. From this vantage point you can really appreciate the beautiful sweep of this white sand bay. While it is possible to drive about 5 miles south on the beach, the auto exit ramp lies 1 mile to the south.

Leaving Pismo Beach, follow highway 1 south, passing flat wide fields of vegetables and eucalyptus groves through GUADALUPE, a rather poor argricultural town. The road becomes a divided two-lane highway as the 135 and 1 merge. After passing the gates of Vandenburg Air Force Base (as you approach Lompoc), take a left turn onto Mission Purisma Road which leads to MISSION LA PURISMA CONCEPCION founded in 1787 and now carefully restored and maintained by the State Park system. A self-guided tour offers you the opportunity to see how the Indians practiced mission crafts such as leatherworking, candlemaking and building. The simply decorated church with its sparse furnishings, rough floors and stenciled walls is typical of Spanish and Mexican churches of the period. One of the nicest aspects of La Purisma Concepcion Mission is its lovely setting - far in the countryside amidst rolling hills and meadows filled with flowers.

Leaving the mission, follow signs for BUELLETON which has the redoubtable fame of being the home of split pea soup. Standing just before the 246 crosses the 101 is Andersen's Pea Soup Restaurant. The menu has more to offer than soup, but it is still possible to sample a bowl of the food that put this little community on the map.

From Buelleton it is just a short drive into SOLVANG, a town settled originally by

Danish immigrants that has now become a rather Disneyfied version of how the perfect Danish village should look - a profusion of thatch-like roofs, painted towers, gaily colored windmills and cobblestoned courtyards. The shops house a plethora of calorific bakeries, fudge and candy stores interspersed with nifty-gifty Scandinavian craft shops. Interestingly enough, a large portion of the town's residents truly are of Danish descent. Even if you are not in the mood for shopping the town merits a bakery stop.

Leaving Solvang, rejoin highway 246 and follow signs for Santa Barbara, your destination for tonight. Just outside Santa Inez the 246 merges with the 154 and the lush green valley gives way to hills as the road climbs up the San Marcos Pass through the mountains. Rounding the crest of the pass, you see Santa Barbara spread before you hemmed between the mountains and the sea. The red tile roofs and the abundance of palm trees add an affluent look to this prosperous town.

Your recommended lodging for your stay in Santa Barbara is THE CHESHIRE CAT, occupying two elegant Victorian houses on a quiet suburban street a short drive from the center of town.

The Cheshire Cat
Santa Barbara

The theme of The Cheshire Cat, "Alice in Wonderland", is created by a set of porcelain storybook figurines which are displayed in the dining room. Each of the bedrooms also carries out the "Alice in Wonderland" motif, with most of the rooms named for a character. The guest rooms, prettily decorated in Laura Ashley papers and fabrics, are especially inviting. On sunny days breakfast is served on white tables dressed with pretty pink cloths on the brick patio between the two houses.

SANTA BARBARA is one of California's loveliest cities. The homes, commercial offices and public buildings show a decidedly Spanish influence and make such a pretty picture - splashes of whitewashed walls, red-tiled roofs and palm trees snuggled against the Santa Ynez mountains to the east and stretching out to the brilliant blue waters of the Pacific on the west.

A pleasant introduction to Santa Barbara is to follow the scenic driving tour which is outlined in the brochure published by the Chamber of Commerce (you can probably pick one up at your hotel). The route is well marked and gives you an overall glimpse of the city as you drive by beaches, the wharf, the old downtown area and affluent suburbs. The brochure also outlines what is called the "Red Tile Walking Tour" which guides you through the beautiful streets of Santa Barbara. It will take discipline to stay on the path as you pass the multitude of shops filled with so many tempting things to buy, but do continue on, because Santa Barbara is a beautiful city whose public buildings are lovely. The highlight of the tour is the Santa Barbara County Courthouse, a magnificent adobe structure with a Moorish accent.

You definitely must not leave town without visiting the splendid MISSION SANTA BARBARA which is located at the rise of the hill on the northern edge of town. This beautiful church with two bell towers faces a large park laced with rose gardens. As in many of the other missions, although the church's main purpose is for religious services, a museum is incorporated into the complex with examples of how life was lived when the Spaniards first settled in California.

When your allotted stay in Santa Barbara draws to a close, it is a little less than a 100-mile drive to the greater Los Angeles area. The vast, often smog-filled, Los Angeles basin is crisscrossed by a mind-boggling network of freeways that confuses all but the resident Southern Californian. Frustrating traffic jams at the morning and afternoon rush hours are a way of life. Therefore, plot the quickest freeway route to your destination and try to travel during the middle of the day in order to avoid the worst traffic. Unlike San Francisco and Santa Barbara, Los Angeles does not offer a good selection of pretty, small inns. But there are many nice, modern places to stay. The city is so sprawling that our suggestion is to decide what sights in town you want to be closest to and choose an appropriate motel or hotel. There are many hotel/motel chains offering a wide selection of places to stay from the simplest motel to the most luxurious of hotels. Call and find out what is available closest to where you want to be - whether it is Hollywood, Beverly Hills, Disneyland, Santa Monica, Pasadena or right in the heart of the city.

The greater Los Angeles area has an incredible wealth of places to visit and things to do - something to suit every taste. Sightseeing suggestions begin on page 31.

WEATHER WISE: San Francisco and the coast beyond Big Sur is often foggy during the summer months and cool and rainy during the winter. In southern California the weather is warmer year round and less rain falls during the winter. Smog is a problem in certain parts of the Los Angeles area during the summer.

Leisurely Loop of Southern California

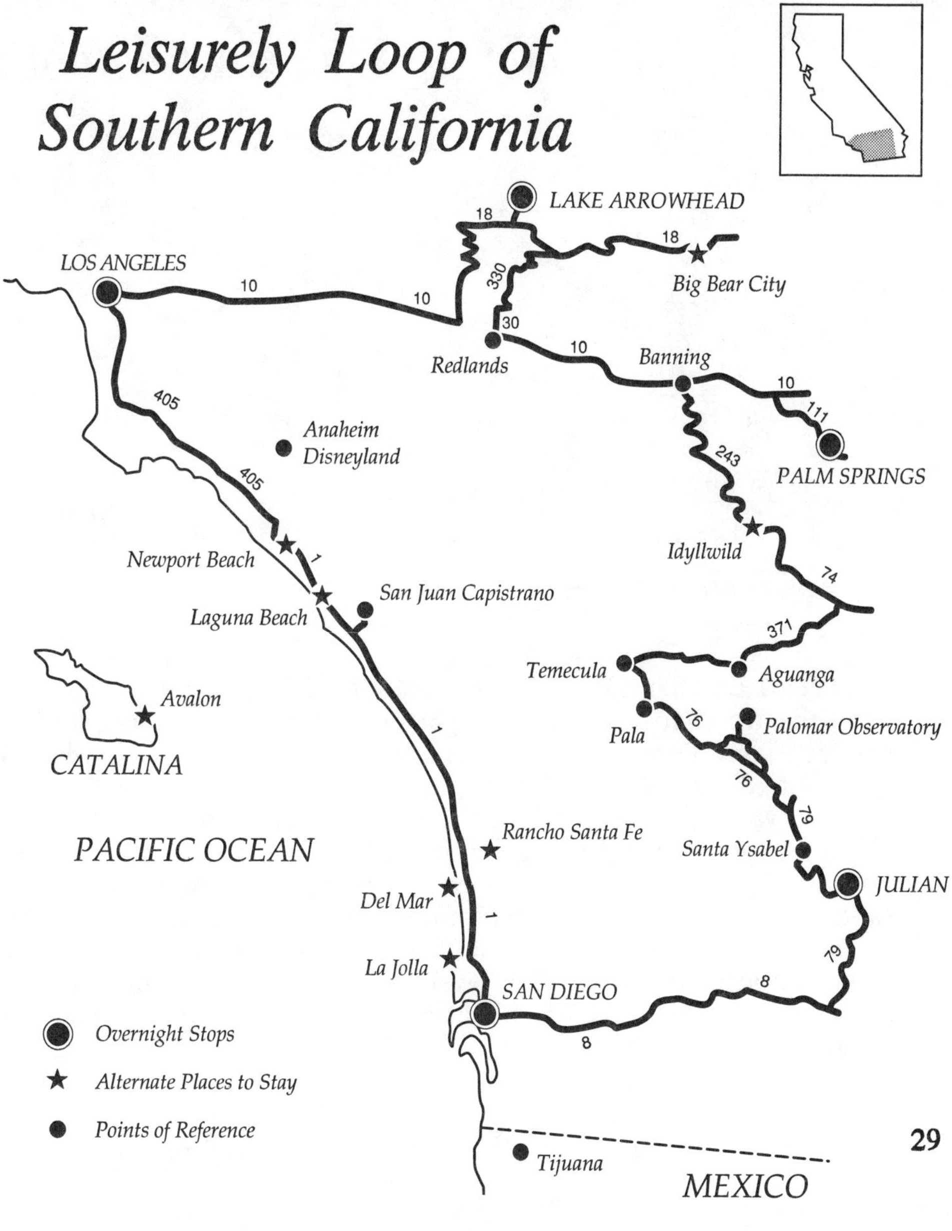

Leisurely Loop of Southern California

Mission San Diego De Alcala

Los Angeles and San Diego are popular destinations, attracting travellers from around the world to a wealth of sightseeing treats. But, in addition to visiting these justifiably famous cities, we hope to entice you to venture out into the countryside to explore lesser known sightseeing gems: quaint Balboa Island with its handsome yachts, charming La Jolla with its idyllic beaches, picturesque Julian exuding its gold rush heritage, secluded Idyllwild nestled in the mountains, glamorous Palm Springs where movie stars still hide away, beautiful Arrowhead with its crystal clear lake. Perhaps nowhere else can you discover within only a few brief miles such a fabulous fabric of places to visit - all so different, all so appealing. White sand beaches, forests with towering pines, deserts rimmed with snow-peaked mountains, bountiful orchards, historical mining towns, and shimmering blue lakes - all await your discovery.

When considering your hotel choice, remember that LOS ANGELES is an enormous metropolis, a hodgepodge of city and suburbs, connected by an overwhelming maze of very busy freeways - during the commuter rush hours it can take hours to get from one side of the city to the other. Consequently we suggest that you choose a hotel close to what you want to see and do. Unfortunately, Los Angeles does not offer a wide selection of inns. However, there are many hotels and motels - some quite outstanding.

If you are going to be staying for an extended period of time in Los Angeles, supplement this guide with a book totally dedicated to what to see and do. There is also a wealth of free information available from the Los Angeles Visitors' Bureau (213) 624-7300 - they will send you a very useful packet of information. We are not going to try to describe in detail all the greater Los Angeles area sightseeing possibilities, just briefly mention a few highlights.

DISNEYLAND: The wonderland created by Walt Disney needs no introduction. What child from 2 to 92 has not heard of this Magic Kingdom inhabited by such lovable characters as Mickey Mouse, Donald Duck, Pluto and Snow White? The park is a fantasy land of fun, divided into various theme areas. You enter into Main Street U.S.A. and from there it is on to Tomorrowland, Fantasyland, Frontierland and Adventureland - each with its own rides, entertainment and restaurants. Disneyland is open every day of the year. The park is located at 1313 Harbor Boulevard in Anaheim. For further information call (714) 999-4565.

HUNTINGTON LIBRARY, ART GALLERY AND BOTANICAL GARDENS: The home and 207-acre estate of the late Henry Huntington is open to the public and should not be missed by any visitor to the Los Angeles area. Huntington's enormous home is now a museum featuring the work of French and English 18th-century artists. What makes the museum especially attractive is that the paintings are displayed in a home-like setting surrounded by appropriately dramatic furnishings. Nearby, in another beautiful building, is the Huntington Library - a real gem containing, among other rare books, a 15th-century copy of the Gutenberg bible, Benjamin Franklin's handwritten autobiography and marvelous Audubon bird prints. The gardens of the estate merit a tour in themselves and include various sections such as a rose garden, a Japanese garden, a camelia garden, a cactus garden, an English garden and a bonsai garden. Located at 1151 Oxford Road in San Marino, the estate is open Tuesday through Sunday from 1:00PM to 4:30PM. If you plan to visit on a Sunday, you must call ahead to make a reservation at (818) 405-2141. For further information call (818) 405-2100.

J. PAUL GETTY MUSEUM: Even non-art enhusiasts enjoy the J. Paul Getty Museum, a replica of an ancient Roman villa from Herculaneum, dramatically set in 10 acres of garden. The reflecting pool, bronze statues and marble columns add to the grandeur of this very special museum which features many Greek and Roman sculptures and an excellent collection of 18th-century European art. Either a taxi must drop you off at the front gate or you must call ahead to make a parking reservation - you cannot just walk up to the museum. The museum is located at 17985 Pacific Coast Highway, Malibu, open Tuesday through Sunday from 10:00AM to 5:00PM. For further information call (213) 458-2003.

NBC TELEVISION STUDIOS: Los Angeles is the television capital of the world. To get an idea of what goes on behind the screen, visit the NBC Television Studios and take their one-hour tour which gives you a look at where the stars rehearse, how costumes are designed, how stage props are made and what goes into the special effects. The tour also visits some of the show sets. The Studios are located at 3000 West Alameda Avenue in Burbank. For further information call (818) 840-3537.

THE NORTON SIMON MUSEUM OF ART: The Norton Simon Museum of Art is without doubt one of the finest private art museums in the world, set in a beautiful Moorish-style building accented by a reflecting pool and manicured gardens. Norton Simon and his actress wife, Jennifer Jones, share their incredible collection of art including paintings by such masters as Rubens, Rembrandt, Raphael, Picasso and Matisse. The museum, open Thursday through Sunday from noon to 6:00PM, is located at 411 Colorado Boulevard in Pasadena. For further information call (818) 405-2100.

PUEBLO DE LOS ANGELES: With all the tinsel of modern-day Los Angeles, it is easy to forget that this city grew up around a Spanish mission. You catch a glimpse of the town's history in Pueblo de Los Angeles, a little bit of Mexico where Hispanic people sell colorful Mexican souvenirs and operate attractive restaurants. The 42-acre complex of old buildings (some dating back to the 1780s) has been restored and is now a state park. Located at 130 Paseo de la Plaza, Los Angeles. For further information call (213) 628-1274.

THE QUEEN MARY AND SPRUCE GOOSE: If you take highway 710 west to Long Beach, the freeway ends at the waterfront where one entry fee gives access to two major attractions. The first, the Spruce Goose (the largest aircraft ever built), is housed in a giant bubble, with steps leading up to platforms where you can get a good look inside to see Howard Hughes's dream creation built entirely of wood. The Queen Mary is docked alongside: you can go aboard and wander through the biggest ocean liner ever built. A portion of the ship is a hotel, the rest a museum, re-creating the days of splendor when the Queen Mary was queen of the seas.

UNIVERSAL STUDIOS: Visiting Universal Studios, the biggest, busiest movie studio in the world, is like going to an amusement park. Included in the admission price is a 2-hour tram journey that takes you around the 420-acre lot, out of the real world and into make believe. Along the way *Jaws* tries to grab you, the Red Sea parts to let you pass, an Alpine avalanche almost engulfs you and you are attacked by robots. This is an entire day's outing for there is so much to see and do - stunt shows, animal shows, Streets of the World, Star Trek Adventure, and on and on. The studios are just off the Hollywood Freeway at the Universal Center Drive exit in Universal City. For further information call (818) 508-9600.

It takes only a couple of hours to whip down the freeway between Los Angeles and San Diego; instead, follow our sightseeing suggestions and dawdle along the way to enjoy some of southern California's coastal attractions en route.

Drive south from Los Angeles on highway 405, the San Diego Freeway, until you come to highway 73, the Corona del Mar Freeway, which branches to the right toward the coast. Take this, then in just minutes you come to highway 55, Newport Boulevard. Exit here and stay on the same road all the way to NEWPORT BEACH. Soon after crossing the bridge, watch for the sign to your right for Newport Pier. (In case you get off the track, the pier is at the foot of 20th Street.) Try to arrive mid-morning so that you can capture a glimpse of yesteryear when the DORY FLEET comes in to beach (just to the right of the pier). The Dory Fleet, made up of colorfully painted, open wooden fishing boats, has been putting out to sea for almost a hundred years. It is never certain exactly what time the fleet will come in (it depends upon the fishing conditions), but if you arrive mid-morning the chances are you will see the fishermen preparing and selling their catch-of-the-day from the back of their small boats. If seeing all the fresh fish puts you in the mood for lunch, walk across the street to the Oyster Bar & Grill - the food is excellent and the clam chowder truly outstanding. If you want to overnight in Newport Beach, Doryman's Inn, just steps from the pier, is highly recommended.

Newport Beach is on a long, thin peninsula. After seeing the Dory Fleet, continue south: the next community you come to is BALBOA. In the center of town there is a clearly signposted public parking area adjacent to Balboa Pier: leave your car here and explore the area. The beach is beautiful - stretching the entire length of the long peninsula, all the way from the southern tip of land to beyond Newport Pier to the north. Stroll along the beach and then walk across the peninsula (about a two-block span) to the Balboa Pavilion, a colorful Victorian gingerbread creation smack in the center of the wharf. Next to the pavilion are several booths where tickets are sold for cruises into the harbor. One of the best of these excursions is on the Pavilion Queen which makes a 45-minute loop of the bay. Buy your ticket and, if you have time to spare until the boat leaves, wander around the nostalgic, honky-tonk boardwalk with its cotton candy, ferris wheel, saltwater taffy shops and penny arcade. But be back in time to board your boat because the Balboa harbor cruise should not be missed. Along the way is a boat fancier's dream: over 9,000 yachts moored in the harbor. Also of great interest are the opulent homes whose lawns stretch out to the docks where their million-dollar cruisers are moored.

A block from the Balboa Pavilion is the ferry landing - you cannot miss it. After your cruise, retrieve your car and follow signs to the Balboa Ferry. You might have to wait in line a bit because the little old-fashioned ferry only takes three cars at a time. When your turn comes, it is just minutes over to BALBOA ISLAND, a delightful, very wealthy community. Park your car on the main street and poke about in the pretty shops, then walk a few blocks in each direction. The homes look quaint and many seem quite small and simple, but looks are deceiving - the price tags are very high.

From Balboa Island there is a bridge across the harbor to the mainland. Almost as soon as you cross the bridge, turn right, heading south on highway 1 through the ritzy community of CORONA DEL MAR. Although there is still a quaintness to the area, exclusive boutiques, expensive art galleries, palatial homes and trendy shops hint at the fact that this is not the sleepy little town it might appear to be.

From Corona del Mar highway 1 parallels the sea which washes up against a long stretch of beach bound by high bluffs. The area seems relatively undeveloped except for its beach parks. About 11 miles south of Corona del Mar the road passes through Laguna Beach, famous for its many art galleries, pretty boutiques and miles of lovely beach. In summer, from mid-July through August, Laguna Beach is usually packed with tourists coming to see the Pageant of the Masters, a tableau in which town residents dress up and re-create paintings. Two dozen living paintings are staged each evening and viewed by spectators in an outdoor amphitheater.

Continue south along the coastal highway. Soon after passing Dana Point, take the turnoff to the east on highway 5 to SAN JUAN CAPISTRANO. Watch for signs directing you off the highway to MISSION SAN JUAN CAPISTRANO (just two blocks from the freeway). This mission, founded by Father Junipero Serra in 1776, has been carefully restored to give you a glimpse of what life was like in the early days of California. Although located in the center of town, the mission creates its own environment since it is insulated by lovely gardens and a complex of Spanish adobe buildings. Another point of special interest at San Juan Capistrano is that the swallows have chosen it as "home", arriving every March 19th (St. Joseph's Day) and leaving October 23rd.

After visiting the mission, retrace your route to the Coastal Highway and continue south on the 1 to SAN DIEGO, just an hour's drive away. There are several excellent choices of places to stay in San Diego, but because of its prime position (a few blocks west of Balboa Park) and because children are accepted we suggest the BRITT HOUSE, a large, handsome, Victorian mansion.

When you arrive, the owner, Daun Martin, will probably be there to greet you. If not, her assistant, warm and witty Pat, will welcome you in her Cockney brogue and "mother" you throughout your stay. Pat insists you relax for a cup of tea and cake or cookies before you settle into your room. Some of the guest rooms are on the first floor and others are reached up a dramatic staircase lighted by a sensational two-story-high stained glass window. If you want more privacy request the garden cottage. Make reservations well in advance: only one of the guest rooms has a private bathroom.

Britt House
San Diego

You need to allow several days in the San Diego area as there is so much to see and do. Upon request the San Diego Visitors' Bureau, (619) 232-3101, will send you a packet of valuable information. To give you an idea of what is available, some of the favorite tourist attractions are:

BALBOA PARK: Balboa Park is without a doubt one of the highlights of San Diego. If you are staying at the Britt House, it is an easy walk to the park. One of the most famous attractions within the park is the San Diego Zoo, one of the finest in the world. A good orientation of the zoo is to take either the 40-minute bus tour or else the aerial tramway. Most of the more than 3,000 animals live within natural-style enclosures with very few cages. The Children's Zoo is especially fun, with a nursery for newborn animals and a petting zoo. Balboa Park offers much more than its splendid zoo. There are fascinating museums and exhibits within the 1,400-acre park: the Museum of Man, the Aerospace Museum, the San Diego Museum of Art, the Timken Art Gallery, the Natural History Museum, the Reuben H. Fleet Space Theater and Science Center, the Hall of Champions, the Museum of Photographic Arts, the Lily Pond and the Botanical Building. Most of the museums are housed in picturesque Spanish-style buildings.

CORONADO: While in San Diego take the bridge or the ferry over to Coronado, an island-like bulb of land tipping a thin isthmus that stretches south almost to the Mexican border. Here you find not only a long stretch of beautiful beach, but also the Coronado Hotel, a Victorian fantasy of gingerbread turrets and gables. The Coronado is a sightseeing attraction in its own right and makes an excellent choice for a luncheon stop.

THE EMBARCADERO: The Embarcadero is the downtown port area located along Harbor Drive. From here you can take a harbor cruise or visit one of the floating museums tied up to the quay. One of these, the Star of India, built in 1863, is a dramatic tall-masted ship that carried passengers and cargo around the world. Not as old, but also interesting, is the Medea, a turn-of-the-century luxury yacht. For information call (619) 234-9153.

GASLIGHT QUARTER: In the heart of San Diego is the Gaslight Quarter where renovation is still under way to restore the turn-of-the-century buildings. We found this to be a somewhat dilapidated area inhabited at night by some questionable characters lolling about the street corners, but by the time you arrive it may have greatly improved.

HERITAGE PARK: Just adjacent to Old Town is Heritage Park, where some of San Diego's Victorian heritage is preserved. Next to the spacious village green a street lined with fabulous Victorian houses slopes gently uphill. The houses were moved here from other areas of San Diego to save them from the bulldozers. These intricate creations now house small shops and offices (be sure not to miss the doll shop with a wonderful collection of doll houses and antique toys). If you want to stay in old San Diego our recommendation in the area is the Heritage Park Bed & Breakfast.

LA JOLLA: Be sure to visit La Jolla, "The Jewel" - a sophisticated suburb just north of San Diego. Classy shops line the streets and spectacular homes, secluded behind high walls, overlook the ocean. La Jolla is home to a branch of the

University of California and within its Scripps Institution of Oceanography are an excellent aquarium and museum featuring marine life from California and Mexico. However, what really makes La Jolla so special are her beautiful white sand beaches sheltered in intimate little coves. If you prefer to stay here rather than in San Diego proper, The Bed & Breakfast Inn at La Jolla, is highly recommended.

MEXICO: Mexico lies just south of San Diego. Do not judge the many wonders of Mexico by its border town of Tijuana, but if you would like to have a taste of Mexico, take one of the tours which leave from downtown for the short drive to the border. A more interesting possibility is to take a boat daytrip. This avoids the tourist jam of cars at the border and treats you to a view of San Diego Harbor en route. United States citizens need only carry identification such as a driver's license if they are staying in Mexico for less than 72 hours. For further information call Gray Line Tours at (619) 231-9922.

MISSION SAN DIEGO DE ALCALA: The oldest of the chain of Spanish missions that stretched up the California coast is Mission San Diego de Alcala. The mission was originally closer to San Diego but was moved to its present site (10818 San Diego Mission Road) in 1774. To reach the mission head east on highway 8 and it is well signposted to the north of the highway just beyond the intersection of highway 15. For further information call (619) 281-8449.

OLD TOWN: Old Town is where San Diego started. Just southeast of the intersection of highways 5 and 8 you see signposts for the oldest sections of San Diego. The area has been designated as a city park and several square blocks are open only to pedestrians. Make the Historical Museum your first stop and orientate yourself by viewing a scale model of San Diego in its early days. Although small in area, Old Town is most interesting to visit as many of the buildings are open as small museums, such as the Machado-Steward Adobe, the Old School House, and the Seeley Stables (an 1860s stage depot with a good display of horse-drawn carriages). If you are in Old Town at meal time, you will find many attractive restaurants. For further information call (619) 291-4903.

SEAPORT VILLAGE: Just a little way south of the Embarcadero is Seaport Village, a very popular tourist attraction and fun for adults and children alike. Situated right on the waterfront, it has little paths which meander through 23 acres of a village of shops and restaurants built in a colorful variety of styles from Early Spanish to Victorian. Street artists display their talents to laughing audiences. An old-time merry-go-round (an import from Coney Island) jingles its gay melody, irresistibly beckoning children from 2 to 92 to climb aboard.

SEA WORLD: San Deigo's marine display is in Mission Bay Park. Set in an 80-acre park, Sea World features one of California's famous personalities, Shamu, the performing killer whale who delights children of all ages with his wit and aquatic abilities. (Fans of Shamu will be happy to know that there is now a baby Shamu, born on September 23, 1988.) Another wonderful show is the Penguin Encounter where you watch comical penguins waddling about in their polar environment. For further information call (619) 226-3901.

WILD ANIMAL PARK: This is a branch of the San Diego Zoo 30 miles north of the city near Escondido - truly a zoo on a grand scale. The animals roam freely in terrain designed to match their natural habitat. You feel as if you are on a safari in Africa as you watch for lions and other animals while you tour the park on the Wgasa Bushline Monorail tour. There are also several open theaters where animal shows are presented. For further information call (619) 234-6541.

DESTINATION II — JULIAN

Gold rush days are usually associated with San Francisco and the northern California gold rush towns. But the San Diego hills had their brief moment of glory when in the 1870s gold was discovered. The town of Julian remains to tell its history.

Highway 8 takes you east from San Diego and winds through low shrub-filled canyons dotted with ever expanding housing suburbs. About half an hour after leaving the city take a left-hand turn and head north on highway 79. The road weaves through an Indian reservation and the scenery becomes prettier by the minute as you climb into the mountains and enter the CUYAMACA RANCHO STATE PARK. There are not many opportunities to sightsee en route, but if you would like to break your journey you can pause at the park headquarters and visit the Indian museum or visit the museum at the Old Stonewall Mine. Leaving the park, the road winds down into Julian.

As you enter town, watch on the right-hand side of the road for your home for the night, the JULIAN HOTEL. As you step into the lobby you will feel you are stepping into an old-time Western movie. Everything is either authentic to the late 1800s or is a carefully chosen reproduction. You may not have chosen the gaudy floral carpet or some of the mishmash of colors and patterns in the wallpapered guest rooms, but if you had been a guest in the 19th century you would have been welcomed by very similar decor. So appreciate the romance of a bygone era while booking well in advance to secure one of the few rooms with a private bathroom. Interestingly, the Julian Hotel was built by Albert Robinson, a freed black slave from Georgia. Your gracious host, Steve Ballinger, is a rich source of wonderful tales about the town and the hotel.

JULIAN is a small town that can easily be explored in just a short time. What is especially nice is that, although it is a tourist attraction, the town is not "tacky touristy". Rather, you get the feeling you are in the last century as you wander through the streets and stop to browse at some of the antique shops, visit the small historical museum in the old brewery and enjoy refreshment at the soda fountain in the 1880s drug store. If you want to delve deeper into mining, just a short drive (or long walk) away on the outskirts of town is the Eagle Mine - founded by pioneers from Georgia, many of them soldiers who came here after the Civil War. Tours are taken deep into the mine and a narration gives not only the history of the mine, but the history of Julian.

If you are in Julian in the fall, you can enjoy another of Julian's attributes - apples. Although you can sample Julian's wonderful apples throughout the year (every restaurant has its own special apple pie on the menu), the apple becomes king during the fall at harvest time. Beginning in October and continuing on into November, special craft shows and events are held in the Julian Town Hall, and of course apples are featured at every meal. You might also want to visit one of the packing plants on the edge of town where you can buy not only apples, but every conceivable item that has apples as a theme.

Julian Hotel
Julian

DESTINATION III — PALM SPRINGS

(POSSIBLE SUMMER DEVIATION: If you are travelling in summer be forewarned that Palm Springs is hot, very hot, so you might well consider staying over in the cool mountain oasis of Idyllwild instead of Palm Springs. If so, there are delightful places to stay: the Fern Valley Inn, a cluster of quaint cottages tucked into the forest, or the Strawberry Creek Inn, an attractive, wood-shingled bed and breakfast.)

Leave early today so that you can sightsee en route to Palm Springs. It is only a short drive north from Julian on highway 79 to SANTA YSABEL where you turn right at the main intersection. At this junction you see Dudley's Bakery, a rather nondescript looking building that houses a great bakery. Loyal customers drive all the way from San Diego just to buy one of their 21 varieties of tasty bread. As you leave Santa Ysabel you come to MISSION SANTA YSABEL, a reconstructed mission which still serves the Indians. This is one of the less interesting missions but you may want to see the murals painted by the local Indians.

About 7 miles after leaving the mission highway 79 breaks off to the east and you continue north on highway 76. In five minutes you come to Lake Henshaw. Just beyond the lake turn right on East Grade Road which winds its way up the mountain to the PALOMAR OBSERVATORY. Just near the parking area is a museum where you learn about the observatory through photos and short films. It is a pleasant stroll up to the impressive white-domed observatory that houses the Hale Telescope - the largest in the United States. A flight of steps takes you to a glass-walled area where you see the giant telescope whose lens is 200 inches in diameter, 2 feet thick and took 11 years to polish. You cannot see the telescope in operation because it is only used at night, but it is fun to imagine scientists scanning the heavens.

After viewing the observatory, loop back down the twisiting road to the main highway and when it intersects with highway 76 turn right (west), driving through hills covered with groves of avocado and orange trees. In about 12 miles you come to PALA and the MISSION SAN ANTONIO DE PALA, one of the few remaining active *asistancias* (missions built in outlying areas to serve the Indians). This particular one has been in operation since 1810. The mission is small, but the chapel holds great beauty in its rugged simplicity enhanced by thick adobe walls, rustic beamed ceiling and Indian paintings. A bell tower stands alone to the right of the chapel, a picturesque sight; to the left is a simple museum and souvenir shop.

From Pala it is about a ten-minute drive north on S16 to TEMECULA. Just before you enter town the road intersects with highway 79 and you turn right, heading east for

18 miles to AGUANGA where you take highway 371 northeast for 21 miles to highway 74. As you head north on 74 the mountain air becomes sweeter and the scenery increasingly prettier as you enter the forest. In about 12 miles you see signs for IDYLLWILD to your right. Turn here on highway 243 and very soon you come to the small mountain resort tucked into the mountains high above Palm Springs. Homey little restaurants, antique stores and fascinating gift shops make up the town. If you are interested in handmade items stop at MAGGIE'S ATTIC. Originally the store featured handmade items from 15 local artisans. Now Maggie has 750 suppliers, not only from every state, but from around the world. There is also a Christmas section with a marvelous selection of Santa Claus ornaments. The shop is located in an old six-room house at 54380 North Circle Drive.

Leaving Idyllwild, continue north on highway 342 to BANNING where you turn right (east) on highway 10. In about 12 miles you come to highway 111 where you turn right and follow signs to Palm Springs (about a ten-minute drive).

Villa Royale
Palm Springs

To find your recommended lodging in Palm Springs, stay on highway 111 which becomes Palm Canyon Drive as it goes through town. As highway 111 begins to leave town, it makes a sweeping curve to the left and its name changes to East Palm Canyon

Drive. Just after the curve, take the third street on the left, Indian Trail, which brings you to the VILLA ROYALE. You can spot the inn very easily because of the handsome fountain in front. The bedrooms, clustered about a series of intimate courtyards, are all decorated with antiques and each room has its own individual decor reflecting the romance of a foreign country.

PALM SPRINGS is a most appealing destination, a very special location where the splendors of nature are enhanced by hundreds of golf courses whose lush velvety fairways stretch out in every direction into the barren desert, a magnificent combination of colors and textures. Also magnifying the special beauty of Palm Springs is the wonderful contrast of mountains and desert. In the winter you can lounge by the pool tanning in the glorious sun, hear the rustling of the palm trees and yet look up to see snow-capped mountains. It is not only the desert which makes Palm Springs an appealing destination - the town has many attributes: lights cleverly concealed in palm trees which illuminate the main boulevard at night, a wondrous selection of fancy boutiques, beautiful large department stores and small gift shops and a wealth of restaurants offering every imaginable type of food from pizza to gourmet French.

Palm Springs was first discovered by the Indians who came to this oasis to bathe in the hot springs which they considered to have healing qualities. The same tribe still owns much of Palm Springs and rents their valuable real estate to homeowners and commercial enterprises. The hot springs are still in use today.

During the winter season the town is congested with traffic and the sidewalks are crammed with an assortment of people of every age, size and shape dressed in colorful sporty clothes. Palm Springs used to become a ghost town in summer when the days are very hot. However, more and more tourists are coming in June, July and August, attracted by the lower hotel rates. Although the temperature in the summer months is frequently well above 110 degrees, it is a dry heat and not unbearable in the mornings and balmy evenings. In fact, due to the altitude, evenings might even cool down so much that you need a sweater. So, if you visit during the summer, plan your day accordingly: get up early for your sightseeing, spend midday in the comfort of your air-conditioned inn, and venture out again in the late afternoon.

In addition to the pleasures of basking in the sun or playing on one of the many golf courses in the area, Palm Springs offers a variety of sightseeing. The most impressive sightseeing excursion is to take the AERIAL TRAMWAY (located just north of town off highway 111) from the desert floor up 2 1/2 miles into the San Jacinto Mountains. In summer you go from sizzling heat to cool mountain forests while in winter you go from desert to snow. The weather atop the mountain is often more than 40 degrees cooler than in Palm Springs so remember to take the appropriate clothing. At the top there are a restaurant, observation decks with telescopes and miles of hiking trails.

If you enjoy deserts be sure not to miss the LIVING DESERT OUTDOOR MUSEUM (closed in summer) where you follow 6 miles of trails leading through sections which depict different types of desert found in the United States. Do-it-yourself tour booklets are available at the entrance to assist you along the trails.

If you are interested in the rich and famous, join a bus tour which takes you by the outside of their magnificent homes - many movie stars have second homes in Palm Springs.

DESTINATION IV — LAKE ARROWHEAD

Palm Springs is a convenient place to end this itinerary because it is a quick, easy freeway-drive back to Los Angeles. But, if time permits, squeeze in one more contrasting destination, the exclusive Alpine resort of Lake Arrowhead.

Leave Palm Springs and head north on highway 111 for about 10 miles to highway 10 where you turn west for BANNING, passing through rather scruffy desert. About 20 miles past Banning you come to REDLANDS where you exit from the freeway on highway 30 and drive north for a few minutes until you come to highway 38 which you take into the hills. As the road begins to climb up from the valley the scenery becomes prettier with every curve - the dry desert brush is gradually left behind, replaced by evergreen trees. At the town of RUNNING SPRINGS there is an intersection where you turn west on 18. This is called the "THE RIM OF THE WORLD HIGHWAY", a road where sweeping vistas of the valley floor, far below, can be glimpsed through the clouds. Be aware that fog often hovers around this drive and instead of admiring beautiful views you creep along in thick grey mist.

Saddleback Inn
Lake Arrowhead

After about a 15-minute drive, watch for the sign to Lake Arrowhead and follow the road down through the forest to the lake. Just before you reach the lake you see on your left a large tavern-style hotel, the SADDLEBACK INN - your home while exploring this beautiful area. William Rush and Bruce Gelker (the latest owners) have rescued the Saddleback Inn from disrepair and, with love and lots of money, have nurtured it into a sophisticated small hotel. There are a few rooms in the main lodge, but if you are travelling with your family one of the chalets nestled in the forest is a perfect choice. From your hotel it is just a short walk (or drive) down the hill to Lake Arrowhead Village, a newly built cluster of restaurants and shops along the lakefront. Here you can rent boats or, for a fee, enjoy the small sandy beach. Note: there are excellent midweek rates available in Saddleback Inn's cottages.

LAKE ARROWHEAD is bordered by magnificent estates, countryside retreats for the wealthy from Hollywood and Los Angeles. The magnet of Lake Arrowhead is not any specific sightseeing, but rather the out-of-doors. You can take leisurely walks through the forest, picnic in secluded parks, explore the lake by paddle boats or rent bicycles for a bit of fresh-air adventure. You also must take the hour-long ride on the nostalgic steamer which circles the lake - en route the narrator points out the many fabulous holiday homes of the rich and famous.

When it is time to complete your itinerary loop back to Los Angeles, return to the 18, the Rim of the World Highway, and head west. The road follows the crest of the hill and then begins to descend the mountain. As you reach the valley again, watch for signs for Los Angeles and follow highway 10 back into the city. Unless you encounter unexpected traffic, the trip should take about two hours.

WEATHER WISE: The weather along the coast is warm year round and there is very little winter rain. Julian has a more temperate climate - though sometimes in the summer they have the odd very hot day and in the winter the occasional snow shower. Palm Springs can be boiling hot during the summer but is beautiful during the winter. Lake Arrowhead is a mountain resort with warm summer weather and snow in the winter.

Yosemite, the Gold Country & Lake Tahoe

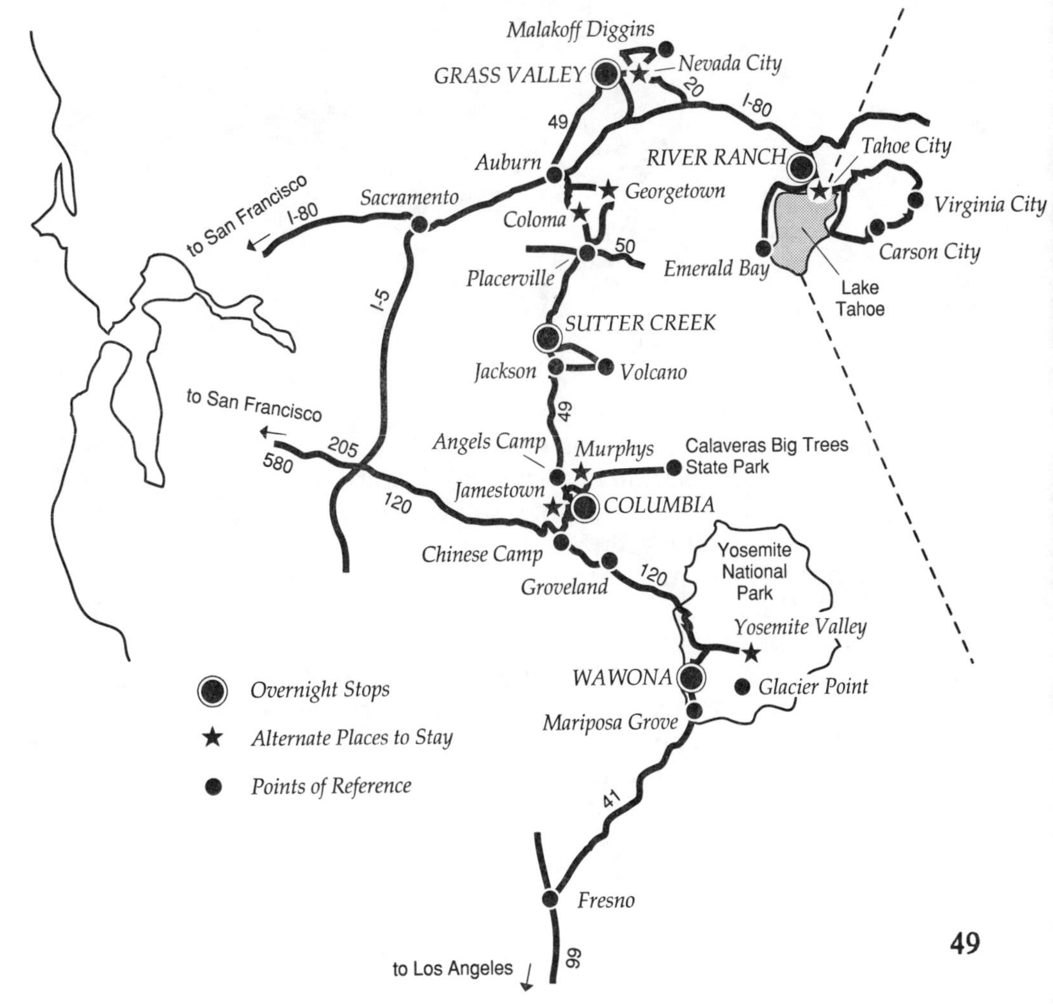

Malakoff Diggins
GRASS VALLEY
Nevada City
20
I-80
49
Auburn
RIVER RANCH
Tahoe City
Georgetown
Virginia City
to San Francisco
I-80
Sacramento
Coloma
Carson City
50
Placerville
Emerald Bay
Lake Tahoe
I-5
SUTTER CREEK
Jackson
Volcano
to San Francisco
49
Angels Camp
Murphys
Calaveras Big Trees State Park
205
580
Jamestown
COLUMBIA
120
Chinese Camp
Yosemite National Park
Groveland
120
Yosemite Valley
WAWONA
Glacier Point
Mariposa Grove
41
Fresno
99
to Los Angeles

Overnight Stops
★ Alternate Places to Stay
Points of Reference

Yosemite, the Gold Country & Lake Tahoe

Nevada City

This itinerary features two of California's most spectacular natural attractions, majestic Yosemite National Park and beautiful Lake Tahoe, and links them together by one of California's best kept secrets - the spirited, nostalgic, gold rush towns which string along the Sierra foothills. These colorful towns date back to 1848 when the cry went up that gold had been found at Sutter Creek, precipitating the rush to California by men eager to make their fortunes. Overnight boom towns sprang up around every mining camp, with a cluster of similar-style saloons, restaurants, hotels, dance halls and homes. Gold rush fever quickly cooled and many of the towns were left, quietly forgotten, until tourists rediscovered their charm. Today these benignly neglected gold rush towns have been spruced up and bustle with activity: antique shops, art galleries, nifty boutiques, attractive restaurants and appealing inns are tucked into the old Victorian houses lining the sleepy streets. The highway that runs through the mother lode country is numbered 49 after the gold-seeking miners who were known as the Forty-Niners.

ORIGINATING CITY — SAN FRANCISCO or LOS ANGELES

As you read through this itinerary, please be aware that each of the areas featured could well be destinations in themselves. Yosemite and Lake Tahoe are especially popular resorts and an entire vacation could easily be dedicated to either one. If that is your desire, just extract from the itinerary the portion that suits your interests. However, the gold rush country is not as well known and makes a super link between Yosemite and Tahoe - or, for that matter, also a great destination in its own right.

Since Yosemite makes a most convenient first-night stop from either San Francisco or Los Angeles, driving directions are given from both so that you can tailor the trip to your own needs.

Much of the first day of this itinerary is spent driving to Yosemite National Park, about a four- to five-hour drive from San Francisco or a six- to seven-hour drive from the greater Los Angeles area. A brief description of what to see and do during your stay in San Francisco begins on page 9 while the attractions of the much larger, more sprawling Los Angeles area begin on page 31.

DESTINATION I — YOSEMITE

From San Francisco to Yosemite National Park is about a four- to five-hour drive. Leave the city over the Bay Bridge, east toward Oakland. Once across the bridge, stay in the middle lane and follow signs for highway 580, heading east, signposted Stockton. Stay on the 580 for about 48 miles until you come to Livermore where highway 580 meets highway 205 which you take continuing east, following signs for Manteca. Near Manteca, take highway 120 east, directly to the northern gate of

Yosemite National Park. Total driving distance is about 200 miles.

From Los Angeles to Yosemite is about a six- to seven-hour drive. Leave the city heading north on highway 5 until you come to the junction of highway 99 which you take north (signposted Bakersfield). Continue on highway 99 to the north edge of Fresno where you take highway 41 north, directly to the southern gate of Yosemite National Park. Total driving distance is about 300 miles.

The main attractions of the over 1,000 square miles of YOSEMITE NATIONAL PARK lie within the narrow 7-mile-long YOSEMITE VALLEY. This stunning monument to the forces of nature is bounded by awesome scraped granite formations - Half Dome, El Capitan, Cathedral Rock, Clouds Rest - beckoning rock climbers from around the world. And, over the rocks, cascading to the valley far below, are numerous high waterfalls with descriptive names such as Bridalveil, Ribbon, Staircase and Silver Strand. Below the giant walls of rock the crystal-clear Merced River wends its way through woodlands and meadows of flowers. Undeniably, this is one of the most beautiful valleys anywhere in the world.

Your first stop should be the information center to obtain pamphlets, books and schedules. The park service offers a remarkable number of guided walks, slide shows and educational programs - look over the possibilities and select the ones that most appeal to you.

Once you are in the valley, park your car and restrict yourself to travel aboard the free shuttle buses as you can do most of your sightseeing by combining pleasant walks with shuttle-bus rides. Alternate modes of transportation are guided horseback trips and bicycles that can be rented. Because the valley is flat, it has miles of paths for biking - a very non-strenuous, efficient way of getting around.

Undeniably, during the summer months Yosemite Valley is jammed with cars and people - spring and fall are much more civilized times to visit.

Within the park, but beyond the valley floor, are many other areas of great natural beauty. Situated just inside the park's southern perimeter is the MARIPOSA GROVE of giant sequoias. It was here that John Muir, the great naturalist who fathered the idea of the national park system, persuaded President Theodore Roosevelt to add the 250-acre grove of trees to the Yosemite park system. A tram takes you through the grove of sequoias and your driver tells the stories of these giant trees - some of the largest in the world.

To the south of the valley highway 41 climbs for about 10 miles (stop at the viewpoint just before the tunnel) to the GLACIER POINT turnoff, a 15-mile drive to a spectacular viewpoint over 3,000 feet above the valley floor. From Glacier Point everything in the valley below takes on Lilliputian proportions: the ribbon-like Merced River, the forest, the meadows and the waterfalls all dwarfed by huge granite cliffs. Beyond the valley a giant panorama of undulating granite presents itself. At Glacier Point rangers offer evening interpretive programs. The ideal photographic time to visit is early in the morning or evening.

A two- or three-night stay in the park is recommended. From hotels through tented cabins, all accommodations in Yosemite are controlled by the *Yosemite Park and Curry Company*: for information call (209) 372-0265. Year round it is necessary that you make your reservations well in advance by phoning (209) 252-4848.

From the stately and very expensive Ahwahnee hotel, through lodges, cabins, tented camps and campsites, Yosemite has accommodations to suit every pocketbook. If your taste in hotels runs to grand, stay at The Ahwahnee. Yosemite Lodge provides more moderately priced accommodations in both cabins and motel/hotel-type rooms. Still less expensive are the tented camps which provide canvas tents on wooden board floors (you do not need sleeping bags since beds and linens are provided). The budget choice is the campsites. But please remember - space is very limited in every category and reservations are essential.

While the attractions of staying in the valley cannot be denied, a more relaxed, serene, country atmosphere pervades at the WAWONA HOTEL, located within the park, but about a 27-mile drive south on highway 41. With its shaded verandahs overlooking broad rolling lawns, the hotel presents a welcoming picture. Bedrooms with private bathrooms are at a premium - most rooms use communal men's and women's bathrooms (sometimes situated quite a distance from your bedroom).

Wawona Hotel
Yosemite

DESTINATION II — COLUMBIA

Leave Yosemite through the northern gate on highway 120 to GROVELAND a handsome, old pine-shaded town. The nearby town of BIG OAK FLAT is little more than a couple of houses strung along the road. As highway 120 drops steeply down 5 miles of twisting road to highway 49, shady pine forests of the mountains give way to rolling, oak-studded foothills, the typical scenery of the gold country.

Heading north on highway 49, detour into CHINESE CAMP, home to over 5,000 Chinese miners in the 1850s and now almost a ghost town sleeping under a profusion of delicate Chinese trees of heaven.

The main street of JAMESTOWN is off the 49 and therefore free of traffic. With its wooden boardwalks, balconies and storefronts, Jamestown has managed to retain much of the feel of the gold rush days. Inviting shops, particularly the emporium, merit a browse, the western-style saloons are full of local color and the Jamestown Hotel has been restored to a beauty such as the gold rush days never witnessed.

Just above Main Street on Fifth Avenue is RAILTOWN 1897 STATE HISTORIC PARK where visitors can see old freight and passenger cars, steams trains and the roundhouse. The park is open at weekends when tours of the roundhouse are conducted.

Leaving town, continue up the main street and cross the 49 onto a peaceful little road that takes you through the countryside to Columbia. Follow signs for Columbia or, wherever a junction is unmarked, continue straight. A 15-minute drive brings you to Parrot Ferry Road on the outskirts of the town.

In the 1850s COLUMBIA was one of the largest towns in California, with many saloons, gaming halls and stores. Today the main street is closed to car traffic and has been restored as a state park to reflect the dusty, raucous days when Columbia was the "gem of the southern mines". The restored buildings are divided between informative exhibits that make learning fun such as the Wells Fargo office, fire station and mining museum, and concession shops where costumed citizens sell goods appropriate to the period. You can enjoy a cold sarsaparilla at the saloon, munch candy rocks at the Candy Kitchen and pan for gold at the mining shack. It is great fun to climb aboard a stagecoach for a ride through the town or take a tour to the Hidden Treasure Mine.

Both the FALLON HOTEL and the CITY HOTEL have been restored (at vast expense) by the state of California to mirror how two of Columbia's hotels looked in gold rush days. The City Hotel on Main Street has a less ornate Victorian decor reflecting the Columbia of the 1860s. The bedrooms off the first floor parlor are the most attractive. While all the rooms have a private toilet and washbasin, showers are down the hall: robes, slippers and a basket to carry your toiletries to and fro are provided. The same bathroom facilities exist at the nearby Fallon Hotel which has been restored to reflect the more fussy, opulent days of the 1880s. You can enjoy theater at the Fallon House Theater adjacent to the hotel. Guests at the City Hotel have the advantage of an excellent restaurant and the lively What Cheer Saloon.

City Hotel
Columbia

DESTINATION III — SUTTER CREEK

Parrots Ferry Road leads north from Columbia, crosses the dam and continues through hilly countryside in the direction of Murphys. If you would like to try your hand at rapelling into the largest cavern in California, the opportunity is afforded you at MOANING CAVERN. You can, of course, take the saner descent down a spiral staircase into a room capable of holding the Statue of Liberty. The rapel is exciting, and with outfitting, instruction and a boost of confidence you descend through a small opening into the well-lit cavern - a most exhilarating experience.

From the caves a short drive brings you to highway 4 where you turn right for about a 20-mile drive to CALAVERAS BIG TREES STATE PARK, a 6,000-acre preserve of forest including two magnificent stands of sequoia trees. A 45-minute self-guided tour takes you through the North Grove and the nearby visitors' center provides information and history on these mammoth trees. If you have time and interest you can visit the more distant South Grove of giant sequoias.

Leaving the park, retrace your route down the 4 and detour into MURPHYS, a sleepy gold rush town sheltered under locust and elm trees where several old buildings and an Old Timers Museum reflect its gold rush heritage. Well signposted from the center of town is another cavern complex, MERCER CAVERNS, with rooms of stalactites, stalagmites and other interesting limestone formations.

At the junction of highways 4 and 49 sits ANGELS CAMP, a pleasant town with high sidewalks and wooden-fronted buildings. Today Angels Camp's fame results not from mining, but from the frog-jumping contests held every May. There is even a monument to a frog taking the place of honor on the main street along which almost all the shops sell items carrying a frog motif.

Leave Angels Camp travelling north on highway 49 through SAN ANDREAS where nearly all evidence of gold rush days has been obliterated by modern shopping centers and commercial businesses. On the outskirts of the town the 49 makes a sharp right turn, signposted Jackson. A 7-mile drive brings you to MUKULUMNE HILL which in its heyday was one of the more raucous mining towns, though now it seems to be quietly fading away. Turn off the 49 and loop through town past the impressive (though genteelly shabby) Hotel Leger and turn left in front of the crumbling I.O.O.F building, then through the residential area and back onto the main road.

JACKSON still supports a population roughly the same of that it had during the gold rush - consequently modern shopping centers and sprawling suburbs are the order of the day. Turn right at the first stop sign in town and almost immediately left to the main street. Set above the old town in an impressive Victorian home is the AMADOR COUNTY MUSEUM, 225 Church Street. The various rooms have rather eclectic exhibits from the gold rush days: for example, the kitchen is full of 19th-century cookware while a small upstairs bedroom displays Indian baskets. Set in an adjacent building is a scale working model of the North Star Stamp Mill that crushes tiny stones.

Retrace your route to where you turned off the 49 and turn left on the 88 signposted for Lake Tahoe and Pine Grove. Just outside PINE GROVE turn left (signposted for your next two destinations, Indian Grinding Rock State Park and Volcano) and follow one of the gold country's prettiest backroads to CHAW'SE INDIAN GRINDING ROCK STATE PARK. A giant slab of limestone has over 1,000 grinding mortars worn in it by Indian women grinding acorn meal. A typical Miwok village has been built nearby with a ceremonial roundhouse and various tree bark dwellings. The adjacent cultural center, built in the style of an Indian roundhouse, has interesting displays from several local Indian tribes.

Just a short drive takes you past the turnoff for Sutters Creek and into VOLCANO, one of the smallest (population 100), prettiest gold country towns that boasted the first lending library and theater group in the state. Now it is a tiny one-street town whose most impressive building is the three-storied, balconied St. George Hotel. Several weathered building fronts give an impression of what the town looked like in more prosperous days. Three miles beyond the town lies DAFFODIL HILL where over 250,000 daffodil bulbs provide a colorful spring display.

Follow the narrow wooded ravine alongside Sutter Creek as it twists down to the town of the same name. SUTTER CREEK rivals Nevada City as the loveliest of the gold rush towns. Its main street is strung out along the busy 49 but somehow the noisy logging trucks, commercial and car traffic do not detract from its beauty. False wooden store fronts support big balconies that hang over the high sidewalks of the the town. Today many of the quaint wooden buildings are home to antique, craft and gift shops.

At either end of the town, set amidst green gardens behind white picket fences, are a handful of lovely New England-style homes. You cannot fail to miss THE FOXES, your recommended country inn for tonight's stay, sitting in its neat green garden at the far end of the main street. Pete and Min Fox have filled their home with every kind of fox motif imaginable - a display case by the front door holds a large part of their collection. Choose from six luxurious suites, each exquisitely decorated and accented by graceful antiques - three are in the main house and three equally lovely rooms in an adjoining annex. Your choice of sumptuous breakfast fare is served to you on silver service in your bedroom. A stay here will thoroughly spoil you.

The Foxes
Sutter Creek

If more contemporary accommodation appeals to you, try THE HANFORD HOUSE just around the corner. Here you find all things "fox" replaced by all things "teddy bear". The rooms with their pine antiques set against stark white walls are most attractive and the "guest register" on the walls and ceiling of the dining room is certainly a conversation starter.

DESTINATION IV — GRASS VALLEY - NEVADA CITY

AMADOR CITY and DRYTOWN, the first two towns you encounter after leaving Sutter Creek as you head towards Placerville on the 49, have an old-world charm and are worth exploring. However, following are a string of commericial towns that offer nothing of attraction to the tourist although the intervening countryside is still most attractive. Follow the 49 as it weaves through the commercial sprawl of PLACERVILLE, crosses highway 50 and climbs out of town.

It is an 8-mile drive along the 49, through apple orchards and woodlands, to Coloma where the gold rush began. Or you can make it a 25-mile drive by taking a right turn just after leaving Placerville onto the 193, a narrow road that twists down a thickly forested canyon to CHILI BAR (a popular spot for rafters to launch) and then does a spectacular weaving climb out of the valley through KELSEY and into GEORGETOWN. Stop to explore Georgetown's shaded streets and then pick up Marshall Road (turn left behind the gas station) which takes you down to the 49 where you turn left into Coloma.

Set on the banks of the American River, the scant remains of the boom town of COLOMA are preserved as MARSHALL GOLD DISCOVERY STATE HISTORIC PARK. It all began in 1848 when James Marshall discovered gold at Sutter's Sawmill. The remaining historic buildings are scattered over a large area, each separated by expanses of green lawn and picnic places along the banks of the

American River. The residential part of town is a sleepy little village of attractive houses set back from the river - it is hard to believe that there was once a population of over 10,000. The museum shows a short film on gold discovery and provides information for a self-guided tour. A duplicate of Sutter's original sawmill, looking like a big shed, sits on the bank of the river. If you would like a change of transportation, a number of companies offer one-day rafting trips on the American River from Coloma.

AUBURN lies a further 20 miles north along the 49 which weaves through its suburbs, crosses the I-80 and continues as a fast, wide road for approximately 24 miles into Grass Valley. An alternate, far more attractive and just a few miles longer route is to take the I-80 north to the Colfax-Grass Valley exit and follow the 174 through pretty woodlands and orchards into Grass Valley. (The following sightseeing suggestion, Empire Mine State Park, is signposted on your left as you near town.)

GRASS VALLEY has a booming economy and sprawls far beyond its historic boundary. Its combination of old downtown buildings housing everyday stores attests to its prosperity. Save town explorations for adjacent Nevada City and concentrate on Grass Valley's EMPIRE MINE STATE PARK at the southern end of town. This hard-rock mine produced $100,000,000 of gold before it closed. An exhibition depicts the mining methods used by miners who came here from the Cornish tin mines in England. Park personnel offer tours of the mine buildings, the most interesting of which is the opulent home of William Bourne, the mine's original owner.

Your recommended lodgings, MURPHY'S INN, is Grass Valley's most attractive Victorian, its porch decorated by carefully clipped ivy. The bedrooms have been restored to their original Victorian grandeur in a most appealing, non-fussy way. Innkeeper Marc and his family live across the street and encourage guests to make themselves at home - in the kitchen he keeps the fridge well stocked with drinks and goodies. The small pool, off the back verandah, is just large enough for a dip.

Murphy's Inn
Grass Valley

The adjacent town of NEVADA CITY is as handsomely quaint as Grass Valley is functional. The old mining stores and saloons have been cleverly converted into pleasant restaurants, antique stores and the like. It is a most attractive town in which to wander about. Many of the settlers here came from the East bringing with them the beautiful deciduous trees of their home states and thus Nevada City is one of the few places that has lovely fall foliage.

As a conclusion to your gold country explorations take a 45-mile round trip to MALAKOFF DIGGINS where high-powered jets of water were blasted at a mountainside to extract gold. The method was very successful, but it clogged waterways for miles and left a lunar landscape where there had once been a forested mountainside. This is a very pleasant summer evening trip, but, rather than run the risk of returning down narrow country roads in the dark, make the loop as you leave Nevada City for Lake Tahoe. The route is quite well signposted but it gives you reassurance to have the map from Nevada City Chamber of Commerce in hand. Leave Nevada City going north on highway 49, following it through wooded countryside for 11 miles to the marker directing you right to Malakoff Diggins (signposted Tyler Foote Crossing Road). The narrow paved road leads you through the forest and, just as you are beginning to wonder quite where you are going, a signpost directs you right down a dirt road into NORTH BLOOMFIELD, a town of white painted houses and buildings set behind picket fences under forest shade. (The town is being restored by the park service and the museum/ranger station is a useful informational stop.) The road through town leads to the diggins proper, a vast lunar landscape of awesome scars. If the weather is inclement, turn back at this point and return to Nevada City by way of the paved highway. Otherwise, continue along the well-maintained dirt road (forking left and downhill at junctions) that winds you through some lovely scenery down to a narrow wood and metal bridge spanning a rocky canyon of the South Yuba River where you pick up the paved road that brings you back to highway 49 on the outskirts of Nevada City.

DESTINATION V — LAKE TAHOE

Leave Nevada City on highway 20 east, a freeway that soon becomes a two-lane highway passing through forests and along a high ridge that gives vistas of the Sierras. As the 20 ends, take I-80 towards Truckee, a fast freeway that climbs into the Sierra mountains through ever more dramatic rugged scenery.

The freeway climbs over Donner Pass and by Donner Lake named in honor of the group of settlers led by George Donner who in 1846 became snowbound while trying to cross the Sierra Nevada in late fall. Harsh conditions and lack of food took many lives and survivors had to resort to cannibalism.

Take highway 89, the Tahoe City exit, and follow it alongside the rushing Truckee River to RIVER RANCH, the hotel suggested for your stay in Tahoe. While the public rooms exude the feel of a mountain resort, the bedrooms, most with iron and brass beds and country decor, have a cozy-country inn feel - quite the nicest rooms have private balconies overlooking the patio and the river. There are many splendid eating places in and around the 3-mile-distant Tahoe City; River Ranch also has a charming restaurant, while the bar is especially well patronized by the apres-ski crowd during the winter. In summer it is great sport to sit on the patio and watch rafters hurtling down the last stretch of their river ride and scrambling ashore: you may even be tempted join them - the Truckee is usually a very gentle river making rafting a fun adventure.

River Ranch Tahoe

After checking into your hotel, follow the Truckee River to its source, LAKE TAHOE. Tucked in a high valley, Lake Tahoe is a vast, blue, icy-cold lake ringed by pine forests and backed by high mountains. (The lake has about 70 miles of shoreline, a maximum depth of 1,645 feet and a summer temperature of about 65 degrees.) When people from the San Francisco Bay Area say they are "going to the mountains", Tahoe is usually where they come. While certain enclaves have their share of hot dog stands, MacDonalds and glitzy gambling casinos, there are many, many areas where this is frowned upon and you can enjoy the exquisite beauty of the lake and its surrounding stunning scenery.

TAHOE CITY combines rustic, folksy shops, restaurants and everyday stores with two quite interesting tourist attractions: Fanny Bridge and the Gatekeeper's Cabin. FANNY BRIDGE is very close; just turn right at the supermarket, and there it is. You will see immediately the derivation of "Fanny" Bridge when you see the tourists leaning over the railing to watch the trout gobble up the food tossed to them. On the same side of the bridge where the fish feed, outlet gates are opened and shut to control the level of the lake - the entire flow of water exiting from Lake Tahoe is regulated here as the water runs into the Truckee River. The other attraction of Tahoe City, the GATEKEEPER'S CABIN, sits on the bank of the Truckee River. The rustic old cabin, once home to the man who controlled the river level, is now an attractive small museum operated by the local historical society.

Hugging the shoreline, highway 89 opens up to ever more lovely vistas as the road travels south. Nine miles south of Tahoe City brings you to SUGAR PINE STATE PARK with its many miles of hiking trails, camping and picnic sites. In summer you can tour the nicely furnished Ehrman Mansion, once the vast lakeside summer home of a wealthy San Francisco family.

You will know by the sheer beauty of your surroundings when you are at EMERALD BAY. The road sits hundreds of feet above a sparkling, blue-green bay and miles of Lake Tahoe stretch beyond its entrance. Center stage is a small wooded island crowned by a stone tea house. A 1 1/2-mile trail winds down to the lake - it seems a lot farther walking up - and in summer you can tour VIKINGSHOLM, the 38-room lakeside mansion built in 1929 and patterned after a 9th-century Norse fortress. It is the finest example of Scandinavian architecture in America and is filled with Norwegian furniture and weavings.

Just below Emerald Bay a trail leads from the parking lot up a 1/4-mile steep trail to a bridge above the cascading cataract of EAGLE FALLS which offers fantastic views of Lake Tahoe. A mile farther up the trail is Eagle Lake, in an isolated, picture-perfect setting.

A memorable outing from Tahoe is a day trip to Nevada's silver towns Virginia City and Carson City. Leaving Tahoe City, follow the northernmost shore of the lake across the Nevada state line and take highway 431 from Incline Village over Mount Rose to the stoplight at highway 395. Cross the highway and go straight ahead up the winding Geiger Grade, highway 341, to VIRGINIA CITY. Built over a honeycomb of silver mines, in its heyday Virginia City had a population of over 30,000. Its wooden sidewalks, colorful saloons (you must visit the Bucket of Blood Saloon) and false-front buildings with their broad balconies make it a town straight out of a John Wayne movie. The stores sell everything from homemade candy to western boots and several have been reconstructed as museums. You can walk up to the old cemetery, take a steam train ride or tour a mine.

Continue through town through Gold Hill and Silver Hill to highway 50 where you turn right for the 7-mile drive to CARSON CITY, the state capital. The town itself has little of interest except for the NEVADA STATE MUSEUM - just across the street from the Nugget Casino on the main road. The highlight of the museum is the re-created silver mine in the basement. You walk along rail car lines in semi-darkness, past exhibits of miners at work and mine machinery - a lot safer than going down a working mine.

To return to Tahoe go south on highway 395, the main street of town, to highway 50 west. Turn right and when you come to Lake Tahoe turn right, following the lake to Tahoe City.

Leaving Lake Tahoe it is a fast four- to five-hour freeway drive, via the I-80, to the San Francisco Bay area. If you are going to Los Angeles take the I-80 to Sacramento and the I-5 south to Los Angeles, a fast eight- to nine-hour drive.

WEATHER WISE: Heavy snow is the norm at Tahoe and Yosemite during the winter, while most of the gold rush towns are beneath the snow line and experience heavy winter rains. During the summer months the days are hot in Yosemite and Tahoe and several degrees warmer in the gold country.

San Francisco to the Oregon Border

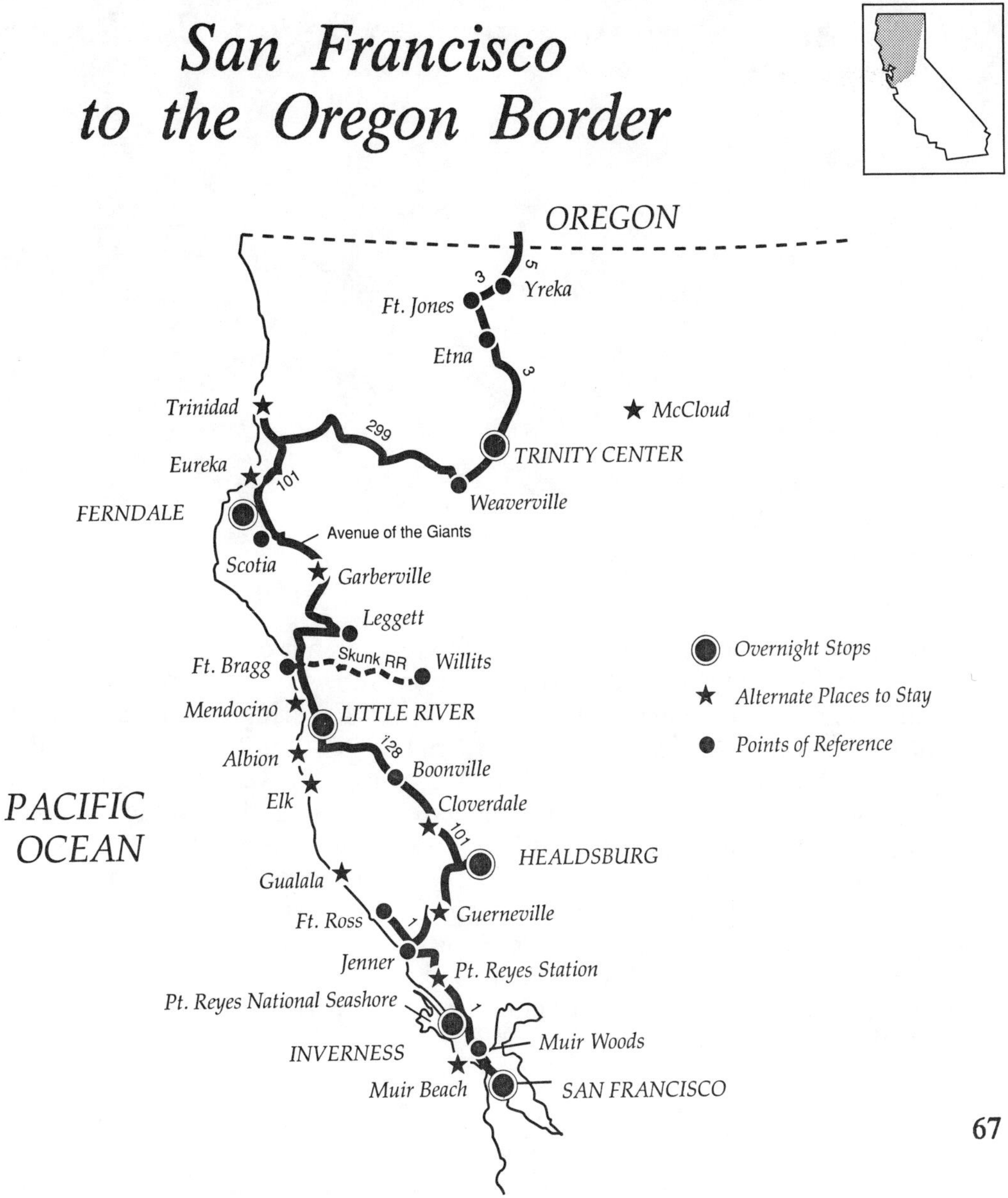

OREGON
5
3
Yreka
Ft. Jones
Etna
3
McCloud
Trinidad
299
TRINITY CENTER
Eureka
101
Weaverville
FERNDALE
Avenue of the Giants
Scotia
Garberville
Leggett
Skunk RR
Willits
Ft. Bragg
Mendocino
LITTLE RIVER
128
Albion
Boonville
Elk
Cloverdale
PACIFIC OCEAN
101
HEALDSBURG
Gualala
Ft. Ross
1
Guerneville
Jenner
Pt. Reyes Station
Pt. Reyes National Seashore
1
INVERNESS
Muir Woods
Muir Beach
SAN FRANCISCO

Overnight Stops
Alternate Places to Stay
Points of Reference

San Francisco to the Oregon Border

Mendocino Coast

If your heart leaps with joy at the sight of long stretches of deserted beaches, rugged cliffs embraced by wind-bent trees, gentle meadows of wildflowers, sheep quietly grazing near crashing surf, groves of redwoods towering above carpets of dainty ferns and mountain hideaways off the tourist route, then this itinerary will suit you to perfection. Nowhere else in California can you travel surrounded by so much natural splendor. Less than an hour after crossing the Golden Gate Bridge, civilization is left far behind you and your adventure into some of California's most beautiful scenery begins. The first part of this route includes many well-loved attractions: Muir Woods, the Russian River, Sonoma County wineries, the Mendocino Coast and the Avenue of the Giant Redwoods. Then the route becomes less "touristy" as it reaches the Victorian jewel of Ferndale and the remote coastal hamlet of Trinidad before climbing into the Trinity Alps with their beautiful mountains and lakes.

ORIGINATING CITY — SAN FRANCISCO

San Francisco, a city of unsurpassed beauty, is a favorite destination of tourists. And it is no wonder. The city is dazzling in the sunlight yet equally enchanting when wrapped in fog. The setting is spectacular: a cluster of hills on the tip of a peninsula. San Francisco is very walkable and if you tire a cable car, bus or taxi is always close at hand. Sightseeing suggestions begin on page 9.

There are many large, super-deluxe hotels in San Francisco plus a marvelous selection of small, intimate inns. Study our various recommendations to see what most fits your personality and pocketbook.

DESTINATION I — INVERNESS

Get a leisurely start this morning in order to miss the commuter traffic. Leave San Francisco on the Golden Gate Bridge following the 101 north. After you cross the bridge pull into the view point for a panoramic view of the city if it is not shrouded in fog.

Continue on highway 101 to the MILL VALLEY exit. Circle under the freeway and follow signs for the 1 north. As the two-lane road leaves the town behind and winds up through the trees, watch closely for a sharp right turn to MUIR WOODS. The road takes you high above open fields and down a steep ravine to the Muir Woods entrance and car park. A park volunteer gives out a map and information and there is no charge for admission to the park. Near the park entrance a cross section of a trunk of one of the stately giant coastal redwoods gives you an appreciation of the age of these great trees as notations relate the tree's growth rings to significant historical occurences during the tree's lifetime: 1066 - the

Battle of Hastings, 1215 - the Magna Carta, 1492 - the discovery of America, 1776 - the Declaration of Independence. But this tree was only a baby - some date back over 2,000 years. Your brochure guides you around the walk beneath the redwoods or you can take a guided tour with one of the rangers. Allow about an hour for the park, longer if you take a long walk or just sit on one of the benches to soak in the beauty.

Leaving the park continue west to the coastal road highway 1. Turn left and almost immediately right. There is a small sign, marked MUIR BEACH, but it is easy to miss. Just before you come to the beach you arrive at the PELICAN INN, a charming recreation of an English pub which fortunately also offers lodging. The food is very good and the ambiance most inviting so we suggest this as a lunch stop. If after lunch you are in the mood for a short walk enjoy the adjacent Muir Beach, a small half-moon beach, bound at each end by large rock formations.

Return to highway 1 and head north along a challenging, winding section of this beautiful coastal road. The road descends to the small town of STINSON BEACH where by entering the state park you can gain access to a fabulous stretch of wide white sand, bordered on one side by the sea and on the other by grassy dunes. This is a perfect spot to stretch and enjoy a walk along the beach.

Leaving Stinson Beach, the road curves inland bordering BOLINAS LAGOON, a paradise for birds, and then leaves the water and continues north for about 10 miles to the town of Olema. At Olema you leave highway 1 and take the road marked to INVERNESS, just a short drive away. When you reach Inverness, drive through the tiny village. Just as you start to leave town you will see on your left the Inverness Cafe, opposite which is posted a sign for THE DANCING COYOTE BEACH. Take this small lane which runs down from the road and ends up at a row of cottages tucked into the trees next to the bay. Each of the cottages is similar, with a living room and small kitchen downstairs and upstairs a bedroom with a skylight so you can watch the stars at night. There is no old-world ambiance - the cottages are relatively new - but the decor is very attractive and the setting just lovely. Also, the location is superbly convenient: Point Reyes Park begins just on the outskirts of town.

There are several choices of good restaurants in Inverness, or, if you want a special treat, it is about a ten-minute drive into the town of Point Reyes Station where the Station House restaurant offers delicious meals. They do not take reservations, but you can put your name in for a table, and then if you need to wait, stroll through the little town.

The Dancing Coyote Beach
Inverness

If the weather is fine and warm allow two nights in the area to give you a full day to explore POINT REYES NATIONAL SEASHORE, a spectacular wilderness area stretching along the sea. If you happen to be here on a weekend, call ahead (415) 663-1200 to find out what special field trips from a choice such as tidepool studies, birdwatching and sights and sounds of nature are offered.

The Ranger Station, located in a handsome redwood building at the entrance to the park, has maps, leaflets and specialty books, a museum and a movie theater where a presentation gives interesting information on the park.

A short stroll away from the ranger station is the "earthquake trail" where markers indicate changes brought about by the 1906 earthquake. Also within walking distance is Morgan Farm where horses are raised and trained for the park system.

A drive out to POINT REYES LIGHTHOUSE is a highlight of a visit here only if the weather is not foggy. As you drive for 45 minutes across windswept fields and through dairy farms to the lighthouse you realize how large the park really is. From the car park a 10-minute walk brings you to the viewing area above the steep steps that lead down to the lighthouse. Be prepared: it is like walking down a 10-story building and, once down, you have to come back up! In winter and spring it is a perfect place from which to watch for migrating gray whales.

The cafe at DRAKES BAY, one of the many beaches along this rugged strip of coast, is a perfect place for lunch.

Another very interesting stop is at the JOHNSON OYSTER COMPANY, on Sir Francis Drake Boulevard - you see a sign pointing left to it as you drive toward Point Reyes Lighthouse. Even if you do not like oysters, stop to see the interesting demonstration of how they are cultivated in the bay for 18 months before being harvested.

DESTINATION II — HEALDSBURG

From Point Reyes Station continue north on highway 1. The road winds through fields of pastureland and creameries and then back to the bay where it follows for a while the northern rim of TOMALES BAY, providing lovely vistas across the water to the wooded hills and the town of Inverness. About a 20-minute drive brings you to the village of Marshall and soon after the road heads inland through rolling ranchland bound by picket fences passing the towns of Tomales and Valley Ford before looping west to Bodega Bay and the small town of JENNER. From here it is about a 15-minute drive to your first sightseeing today at FORT ROSS. "Ross" means "Russian" and this is the site where the Russians, in the early part of the 19th Century, built their fort to protect their fishing and fur interests in California.

After browsing through the museum, follow the footpath through the woods and enter the courtyard bounded by the weathered wooden buildings where the settlers lived and worked. Be sure not to miss the pretty Russian Orthodox Chapel in the southeast corner of the compound. When you have finished roaming through the encampment, if the weather is fine, take the lovely walk along the bluffs above the ocean.

Leaving the fort retrace your path to Jenner and follow highway 116 inland along the banks of the RUSSIAN RIVER. This is a lovely stretch of road, passing through dense forests which open up conveniently to offer views of the very green water of the Russian River. (In winter after heavy rains the river can become a rushing torrent - no longer green and tranquil.) On weekends this road is very congested, but midweek and off season this is a very pretty drive. The largest resort along the river is GUERNEVILLE and just a few miles beyond the town you come to the KORBEL WINERY, a picturesque large building banked with flowers. Plan your day so that you arrive by midafternoon since the last guided tour usually leaves at 3:45PM (to be safe, call to double check the schedule: (707) 887-2294). Korbel is famous for sparkling wines and the tour and video presentation are especially interesting. Three Korbel brothers came to this area from Bohemia to harvest the redwoods and ended up harvesting grapes. There is also a tour of the beautiful rose garden nestled on the slope to the left of the winery.

Sampling champagne at Korbel will whet your appetite for additional wines from Sonoma County. Leaving the winery continue for a short distance along River Road watching for a left-hand turn for Westside Road (if you go over the bridge, you have gone too far.) Westside Road winds its way to Healdsburg, your destination for tonight. Along the way this pleasant country road passes vineyards, meadows with cows grazing, pretty apple orchards and several wineries, including HOP KILN WINERY and the nearby J. ROCHIOLI WINERY which are open for tasting until 5:00PM. The architecture at Hop Kiln is very interesting with whimsical chimneys jutting into the sky. As the name implies, the winery was originally used for drying beer hops.

Just before you come to Healdsburg, Westside Road makes a sharp right turn at which point you see (on your left) an arch leading to MADRONA MANOR, perched on a hillock within 8 acres of parklike garden.

Madrona Manor
Healdsburg

This magnificent large Victorian home is an excellent choice for a base while exploring the area. All the rooms in the main house contain Victorian antiques which complement the fabulous gingerbread structure beautifully. Some of the rooms are even furnished with the original pieces. There is also a charming little carriage house where the bedrooms are attractively decorated with carved furniture. Quite the nicest rooms are the two large front rooms in the main house with private balconies that offer magnificent views of farms and vineyards against a backdrop of hills. If the day is hot enjoy a swim in the lovely pool.

The nearby town of HEALDSBURG has an attractive main square lined with little shops and restaurants. If you prefer to be in town refer to the several hotel recommendations listed in the back of the book.

DESTINATION III — LITTLE RIVER

Leaving Healdsburg take the 101 freeway north for the half-hour drive to CLOVERDALE where you take highway 128 heading northwest toward the coast. At first the road twists slowly up and over a rather steep pass. After the summit the way becomes more gentle as you head down into the beautiful ANDERSON VALLEY. Whenever the hills spread away from the road, the gentle meadows are filled with vineyards. The NAVARRO WINERY set amongst fields of grapes is most attractive and offers tasting of its excellent product. As you approach the ocean (about a 60-mile drive from the 101) highway 128 merges with highway 1 and becomes the coastal road.

The first hamlet you come to is ALBION and about five minutes beyond towards the village of LITTLE RIVER you come to HERITAGE HOUSE, a snug 1877 wooden farmhouse painted yellow with a bright red door, and almost completely draped with ivy. This was one of the original inns in California, for years a favorite romantic getaway for guests from the San Francisco area. It has now become so very popular that reservations are usually needed needed far in advance. (If you are a last-minute planner, do not despair because we have several additional recommendations of places to stay in the area.)

Heritage House's setting of lawn, trees and gardens stretching down to beautiful bluffs above the ocean is so spectacular that you may be tempted to end your sightseeing for today right here. This is a sophisticated resort where a coat and tie are appropriate for the evening meal and the room rate includes dinner as well as breakfast. A few of the guest rooms are in the main house, but most are in a variety of cottages with individual names such as Bonnet Shop, Country Store, and The Stable. Each has its own special character and decor and many have fireplaces.

Heritage House
Little River

If you can pull yourself away from the Heritage House, take the 10-minute drive into the charming, New England-style town of MENDOCINO that juts out on a headland into the ocean. Tucked into the many colorful wood-frame buildings are a wealth of art galleries, gift shops and excellent restaurants. Do not let your explorations stop at the windswept town, but venture out onto the adjacent moorland which drops off into the crashing ocean. A visit to Mendocino would not be complete without a walk along the bluffs. In winter there is an added bonus: spouts of water off the shoreline are an indication that a gray whale is present.

Staying in this area you could most successfully be entertained by doing absolutely nothing else but soaking in the splendid rugged beauty of the Mendocino Coast. However, there are some sightseeing possibilities. Just north of the town of Mendocino you come to FORT BRAGG. This is a sprawling commerical town that has little to offer in the way of quaintness and whose big tourist attraction is the SKUNK RAILROAD which runs between Fort Bragg and Willits. During the summer months you can either take the all-day trip which makes the complete roundtrip to Willits, or choose a half-day trip leaving in the morning or the afternoon. The carriages are not pulled by nostalgic steam engine, but, if you like train rides, you will enjoy the trip into the forest. Frankly, you will have already seen lovelier glens of redwood trees than those you will see on the ride, but the outing is fun, especially if you are travelling with children. The train station is easy to find in the center of town just after you pass over the rail tracks. Call ahead for reservations: (707) 964-6371 - you can secure space by using your credit card.

DESTINATION IV FERNDALE

Leaving the Mendocino area continue following the coast north and enjoy a treasury of memorable views: sometimes the bluffs drop into the sea, other times sand dunes almost hide the ocean and at one point the beach sweeps right up to the road. At ROCKPORT highway 1 turns inland and twists and turns its way over the coastal range, passing through glens of redwood trees and forests. In about 30 miles you arrive at LEGGETT. Just before the junction with 101 look for a sign to your right indicating a small privately owned redwood park where you can drive your car through a tree.

From Leggett continue north along 101 signposted for Eureka. Along the route you pass many small stores advertising every imaginable item made from redwood; so if you have always craved to take a 10-foot redwood teddy bear home to Aunt Tilda this is a perfect opportunity to stop and buy one.

Rather than rush up the 101 follow the old highway, called THE AVENUE OF THE GIANTS, that weaves through the HUMBOLDT REDWOODS STATE

PARK. This is a 33-mile-long drive but you can select the most beautiful section by joining the avenue at MERS FLAT. The two-lane road passes a few stores and then glides into a spectacular glen of redwoods. A particularly idyllic section of the forest is at WILLIAMS GROVE where you might want to stop for a stroll.

Nearby is the Humboldt Park Ranger Station and a small museum whose dedicated volunteer staff answers questions and offers displays and a short slide presentation describing the park facilities.

Continue on the Avenue of the Giants. Pass under the freeway and follow signs to the left to ROCKERFELLER FOREST, the oldest glen of redwoods left in the world - some dating back over 2,000 years. The trees are labeled and a well-marked footpath guides you through the forest to the Big Tree, an astounding giant measuring 17 feet in diameter and soaring endlessly into the sky, and also to the Flat Iron Tree (another biggie with a somewhat flattened-out trunk) located nearby in an especially serene grove of trees.

About 10 minutes after rejoining highway 101 exit to SCOTIA. Plan your day carefully because this is a must. The entire town - homes, shops, restaurant, clothing store, school, hotel - is owned by the Pacific Lumber Company, the largest lumber company in the world. The picturesque little redwood homes are dominated by the PACIFIC LUMBER MILL. Drive into town to the museum - a most unusual building resembling a Grecian temple with redwood tree trunk pillars instead of marble. Passes for the tour of the lumber mill are issued here along with a small redwood shingle which gives you instructions for the self-guided tour. You drive to the visitors' carpark and then, like Dorothy in *Wizard of Oz*, you follow the "yellow brick road", a well marked trail, highlighted with yellow arrows, which guides you throughout the factory.

Your first stop is at the hydraulic barker where you stand in a glass-enclosed observation room and watch as the trees are stripped bare of their bark by a water saw which sweeps back and forth over each trunk like a broom, leaving the trunk naked. Steam roars up to cover the windows and the entire building rumbles as the giant tree trunks are sloshed about like toothpicks. The next stop is the saw mill where the trunk is pulled back and forth beneath a giant-sized rotary saw which slices it into large boards. Walking along the overhead ramp, you watch the entire process from the first touch of the saw until the various sized boards are neatly tucked into huge cardboard boxes and bound tightly with metal straps.

Note: The lumber mill is closed on weekends and holidays. Monday through Thursday, the hours are 7:30AM to 10:30AM and 1:30PM to 3:30PM. On Friday, no passes are given out after 2:30PM. It is best to check times in advance of your arrival by calling (707) 764-2222.

Returning to highway 101, about a 10-mile drive brings you to the FERNDALE exit. Ferndale's Main Street is lined with so many gaily painted Victorian houses and shops that you think Walt Disney had a hand in its design. Actually, the townspeople decided on the appropriate colors, and, as a community project, painted the entire town. Not only does the town sparkle with color, but Main Street is a gem, lined with delightful little galleries and stores - a favorite being the irresistible candy shop where you view in the window the hand-dipping of delectable chocolates.

Luckily, one of the finest Victorians in town has been lovingly converted into a small inn appropriately called THE GINGERBREAD MANSION. From Main Street, turn left at the Bank of America, drive one block and you cannot miss the fanciful building of turrets and gables set within a beautifully manicured garden. As you step inside, the parlors and dining room all abound with Victorian-style furnishings. The bedrooms too are old world in decor, but some add a bit of fun such as "his and her" clawfoot bathtubs sitting side by side in the bedroom.

When making reservations at the mansion ask about what special events are featured while you are in town. Many visitors enjoy the small theater on Main Street where some excellent plays are produced.

The Gingerbread Mansion
Ferndale

DESTINATION V — TRINITY CENTER

Leaving Ferndale, retrace your way to highway 101 and continue north through Eureka. About 20 miles beyond the town, take the exit to the coastal hamlet of TRINIDAD. Although the houses are now mostly of modern architecture, Trinidad Bay has an interesting history. It was first discovered by the Portuguese in 1595, claimed by the Spaniards in 1775, flourished in the 1850s Gold Rush as a supply port for the miners and was later kept on the map by logging. Now Trinidad is a sleepy little cluster of homes nestled on the bluffs overlooking a beautiful cove where a wonderfully unsophisticated, untouristy wharf stretches out into the bay. Next to the wharf is the Seascape Restaurant where you can dine on fish straight from the little fishing boats. Stroll along the headlands enjoying the exceptionally lovely views then return to highway 101 and retrace your route 12 miles south to highway 299 heading east. For the first few miles a four-lane freeway cuts through large dairy farms, then the road narrows as it climbs up into the hills. The drive over the mountains is lovely. Especially outstanding is the portion as you head down the eastern side of the pass and follow the Trinity River into Weaverville. Along the river you often see fishermen lazily casting their fly rods and occasionally come across a few lone miners panning for gold.

About two and a half hours after leaving the 101 you come to the picturesque town of WEAVERVILLE, which seems like a stage set for an old John Wayne movie. The museum on Main Street is filled with memorabilia from the Gold Rush days and the JOSS HOUSE belonged to the Chinese who journeyed here in the hopes of finding gold in the Trinity Alps: still in use today, the Joss House is the oldest continuously used Chinese temple in California. Adjacent to the Joss House is a small museum with many photographs which tell poignantly the story of the Chinese people in this part of California.

Carrville Inn
Trinity Center

From Weaverville, take highway 3 north. The road weaves back into the TRINITY ALPS and after a short drive you see segments of Trinity Lake on the right. Toward the north end of the lake you come to the small community of TRINITY CENTER, then 6 miles beyond Trinity Center take the first paved road to your left signposted Carrville Loop, and in a couple of minutes you see your home in the Trinity Alps, the CARRVILLE INN.

What a happy surprise to find such a wonderful little inn tucked into a small valley "in the middle of nowhere". Actually, this now remote spot once bustled with travellers on their way along the popular pass into Oregon. The route through Carrville was a favorite because the Indians were friendly. Barbara and Ray Vasconcellos devoted six years to restoring the historic Carrville Inn Stage Coach stop and they have done a super job - this is one of the finest inns in northern California. The setting is lovely: the simple white house, with a two-tiered verandah stretching across the front, sitting in its own little valley.

There are many hikes you can take from the Carrville Inn. And after one of Barbara's delicious, hearty breakfasts, you might feel compelled to exercise. However, it may be difficult to leave your wicker chair on the verandah where you can soak in the quiet of this little valley.

Explore the Trinity Alps area and when you must leave continue north on highway 3 through the hamlets of Etna and Fort Jones to civilization which returns with a jolt as you reach the outskirts of YREKA and are greeted by a McDonalds, a Taco Bell and a Burger King.

At Yreka, highway 3 intersects with highway 5, an expressway. Turn north here and it is only about 20 miles to the Oregon border. If you are returning to the San Francisco area, a six-hour drive away, follow highway 5 south.

WEATHER WISE: The weather along California's northern coast is unpredictable: beautiful summer days suddenly become overcast when the fog rolls in. Rain falls during the winter and spring; fall really has the most pleasant weather. In the Trinity Alps the summers are warm and snow falls during the winter.

Wandering Through the Wine Country

Old Faithful Geyser

29

128

CALISTOGA

MEADOWLARK

Petrified Forest

Petrified Forest Road

MEADOWOOD

ST. HELENA

Calistoga Road

Santa Rosa

12

29

Rutherford

Oakville

Yountville

Silverado Trail

BELTANE RANCH

GLEN ELLEN

Jack London State Park

29

Sonoma

Napa

12

121

121

29

37

80

to San Francisco

101

to San Francisco

Overnight Stops

Alternate Places to Stay

Points of Reference

Wineries

1 *Trefethen Vineyards*
2 *Domaine Chandon*
3 *Robert Mondavi Winery*
4 *Inglenook Winery*
5 *Rutherford Hill Winery*
6 *Beringer Vineyards*
7 *Hanns Kornell Winery*
8 *Schramsberg Vineyards*
9 *Sterling Vineyards*
10 *Chateau St. Jean*
11 *Kenwood Vineyards*
12 *Glen Ellen Winery*
13 *Buena Vista Winery*
14 *Gloria Ferrer Winery*

Wandering Through the Wine Country

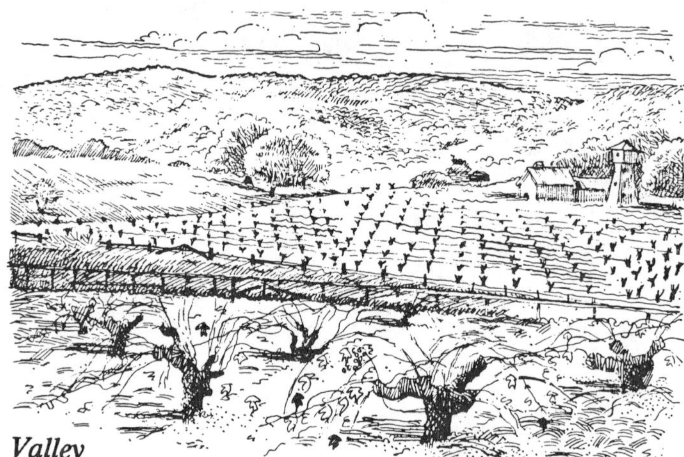

The Napa Valley

The Napa and Sonoma Valleys, just north of San Francisco, have earned a well-merited reputation for the excellence of their wines. Happily for the tourist, many of the wineries are open to the public for tours and tasting. But it is not only visiting the wineries that makes this area so special, these valleys are also memorable for their beauty. A visit to the Wine Country makes a pleasant excursion anytime of year. In summer the days are long and warm, perfect for bike rides, picnics, music festivals, concerts and art shows. As summer days give way to the cooler afternoons and crisp evenings of fall, the lush foliage on the thousands of acres of grapevines turns to yellows, golds and browns - a colorful reminder that it is time for harvest: one can sense the energy of the crush as vintners work against the clock and weather to pick grapes at their prime. In winter, cool days are often washed by rain, but this is also an excellent time to visit since this is "off season" and the tours will be almost private as you travel from one winery to the next. Spring is glorious: mustard blossoms paint the valley yellow - contrasting dramatically with the dark bark of the vines laced with the delicate green of newborn leaves.

ORIGINATING CITY — SAN FRANCISCO

This itinerary is an introduction and a sampling of what the wine country has to offer. The featured wineries have been chosen for a variety of reasons such as their historical interest, the excellence of their wines, the appeal of their tour and their special ambiance. To complement this itinerary, a few inns have been chosen to pace the journey. Visitors to the wine country often spend several days in San Francisco before visiting the Napa and Sonoma wine valleys. Suggestions on sightseeing in San Francisco begin on page 9. This itinerary wends up the Napa Valley and down the Sonoma Valley. Either the Sonoma or Napa wine region can be visited on a day-trip from San Francisco: just extract from the itinerary the portion that suits your interests. Alternatively, rather than move from inn to inn as this itinerary suggests, you can choose a "base" in either of the valleys and set out to follow our sightseeing suggestions.

DESTINATION I — ST HELENA

From San Francisco travel east across the San Francisco - Oakland Bay Bridge. After crossing the bridge, stay in the left-hand lane and follow signs for highway 80 in the direction of Sacramento. Approximately 5 miles after crossing the Carquinez Bridge watch for the Napa/Columbus Parkway (highway 37) turnoff which quickly narrows to a two-lane road. Continue on the parkway to highway 29 which you take in the direction of Napa. The road widens and the scenery improves dramatically as the road nears the base of the Napa Valley. When the road divides again, take the left fork in the direction of Sonoma 12/Calistoga 29 which cuts across the south edge of the valley, across the Napa River. (The right fork (highway 121) goes to Napa and on to Lake Berryessa.) As you cross the bridge, glance north for a lovely, sweeping view of the valley from its widest point to where it narrows in the distance. Highway 29 curves north after the bridge and narrows to a two-lane (in some stretches four-lane) road that travels up the center of the valley from Napa in the south to Calistoga on its northern borders.

Just outside of Napa (off highway 121 and Trancas Street) another road, the Silverado Trail, also travels the length of the valley, hugging its eastern foothills. Highway 29 is the busier road, the address for many of the valley's larger wineries and all the towns. The Silverado Trail, the more scenic, less commercial route, twists and winds amongst smaller vineyards and often offers a welcome escape from the summer crowds and traffic. This itinerary suggests a route north through the Napa Valley, crossing the short distance back and forth between highway 29 and the Silverado Trail, and then travels west to follow a routing south through the Sonoma Wine Valley.

Stay on highway 29 approximately 1/2 mile past the northern outskirts of the town of Napa to Oak Knoll Avenue. Turn east on Oak Knoll, a beautiful drive bounded by almond trees and vineyards, and watch for a small signpost marking the entrance of TREFETHEN VINEYARDS. Surrounded by its own grapes, Trefethen Vineyards is housed in the oldest wooden winery in the Napa Valley. Pumpkin in color with a brown roof, this handsome complex recently celebrated its 100th birthday and there was much reason to celebrate, as the Trefethen family fortunately rescued and lovingly restored the property just over a decade ago. This wonderful old winery was designed by the same architect responsible for the larger and more renowned Inglenook and Beaulieu wineries. Trefethen Vineyards is a delightful, small winery, family-owned and operated, that has proved that size is in no way a factor in excellence. The Trefethens have converted a bulk winery to the production of excellent estate-grown chardonnay, riesling, cabernet sauvignon, pinot noir and eshcol. Trefethen wines are featured in some of the finest restaurants. Old farming implements border the parking area and a brick walk encircles a handsome oak in front of the old winery where you can sample the wines. Tours are available each day at 10:30AM and 2:30PM, but you must make an appointment: (707) 255-7700.

From the entrance of Trefethen Vineyards turn east on Oak Knoll Avenue which jogs north at Big Ranch Road and then continues east to where it ends at the intersection of the Silverado Trail where you turn north. From here the scenery seems only to get prettier as the valley narrows and hugs the eastern foothills. Tucked off this road there are numerous smaller vineyards that are open daily for tasting but offer tours by appointment only: Clos du Val, Stag's Leap Wine Cellars, Pine Ridge and Walt Disney's widow's winery - Silverado.

From the Silverado Trail, turn west at the well-marked Yountville Cross Road. When the road deadends at Yount Road, turn left in the direction of YOUNTVILLE. The road winds round behind town to a stop sign that positions you directly opposite Vintage 1870, a wonderful complex of shops and restaurants housed in a quaint old brick winery. Even non-shoppers will enjoy a stroll through this marvelous old converted winery: the old brick, heavy beams and tiled and cobbled floors are dramatic against a meticulously groomed backdrop of green lawn and flowers. A variety of specialty shops make any purchase possible: toys, antiques, handmade sweaters, books, kitchenware, jewelry or art. An assortment of restaurants will appease most appetites should you desire a gourmet salad, pastries or simply a refreshing ice cream cone. You can also arrange for an early-morning balloon ride - the office for Adventures Aloft (P.O. Box 2500, Yountville 94599, (707) 255-8688), is located opposite Vintage 1870, next to the Vintage Cafe. Departures are at sunrise, the best possible time as the winds are gentle and the air is cool. The flights are expensive, but something to do once and remember forever.

Drive south from Yountville on California Drive, crossing under highway 29 in the direction of the Veterans' Home. Just after passing under the freeway turn right onto the property of DOMAINE CHANDON. When the proprietors of Moet & Chandon first came to the valley with the intention of making sparkling wine following the principles and rigid process of true French champagne, "methode champenoise", they contracted to use Trefethen Vineyards. Successful in their venture, their sparkling wine was well received and they recently moved to the present location and established their own winery called Domaine Chandon. Roses front the vineyards, a French tradition, copied both for its practicality as well as for its aesthetic value. The roses add a grace and beauty to the planted fields, but they are also susceptible to the same root diseases and insect problems. If the roses are blemished, vintners know to investigate the vines closely.

Although the winery is new, mature oak trees shade a lovely lawn and a series of terraced ponds with fountains. A wooden footbridge spans the creek-fed ponds to the stone winery tucked back into the hillside. Tours are offered daily on the hour between 11:00AM and 5:00PM. The visitors' center is closed on Mondays and Tuesdays from October to April: for further information call (707) 944-8844. The tours are hosted by courteous guides who are well informed about the aspects of "methode champenoise". Visitors see first the traditional storage of the wine in polished stainless steel tanks and then continue on to observe the additional steps involved in making champagne. In the cellar bottles of sparkling wine are aged and riddled (turned). In the bottling room you see the process of freezing then disgorging the sediment, corking, cleaning and labeling the bottles. After the tour visitors are invited back to the salon where Domaine Chandon's sparkling wines may be purchased by the glass and enjoyed with complimentary hors d'oeuvres. From the salon it is possible to view through a glass partition Domaine Chandon's elegant restaurant. A visit to Domaine Chandon shows French and Californian vintners, sharing expertise, working side by side in the Napa Valley.

From Domaine Chandon, return to highway 29 heading north a few miles to the roadside town of OAKVILLE. A few buildings comprise this town, the principal one being the original Oakville Grocery. If you plan to picnic, stop here for supplies to accompany your wine-tasting purchases.

The ROBERT MONDAVI WINERY is easy to spot just past Oakville, off the 29, on the left as you travel north. This modern winery was styled after the Franciscan missions, with an open arched entry framing an idyllic view of vineyards. Reservations are advisable: (707) 963-9611. The one-hour tour is extensive, extremely informative and provides a good general introduction to the essence of winemaking. By special arrangement, you can also make reservations for an in depth study, touring the fields and studying the grapes as well as the winery. After each tour guests are invited into the tasting room for complimentary wine tasting. The lovely lawn at back is the site of summer concerts and art shows.

Inglenook Winery

A few miles farther north, just past Niebaum Lane on the left, is the entrance to the INGLENOOK WINERY. From highway 29 you catch only a glimpse of the dormer windows of the original ivy-covered stone cellar set amongst the vineyards. Inglenook, a Scottish term for "warm and cozy corner", is what attracted Gustave Niebaum to this wooded locale in the late 1870s. A Finnish sea captain, Gustave retired from shipping and trading to invest his fortune in winemaking. Inglenook strives to maintain the standards and excellence of its wine as established by the founders. Inglenook is a handsome winery that enjoys a beautiful setting nestled against the western foothills. Dating back to the 19th century, Inglenook is able to offer what the valley's new wineries cannot - character achieved with age and time. A highlight of Inglenook's tour is a walk through the original stone aging cellar containing some magnificent large German oak casks and a tour of Gustave Niebaum's tasting room, modeled after the Captain's cabin on his ship, finished with beautiful carved oak panelling and stained glass windows. Forty-five-minute tours start in the museum area at the entrance and include a movie and wine tasting. Advance reservations are not required, but for further information call (707) 967-3300.

From Inglenook cross highway 29 to Rutherford Road, directly opposite. On the corner are the numerous buildings that comprise BEAULIEU VINEYARDS. Commonly referred to as BV, Beaulieu bottles some excellent wine and now offers both a tour and complimentary tasting. For information call (707) 963-1451.

Rutherford Road affords a scenic drive shaded by an archway of oak trees. Travel the short distance to its end, past the Louis Honig Winery, and then turn north on Conn Creek Road which intersects with the Silverado Trail. Turn north on the Silverado Trail, but drive slowly as you want to take the first right turn onto Rutherford Hill Road which winds up past the famous restaurant and resort hotel, the Auberge du Soleil, to the Rutherford Hill Winery.

Although relatively new, the RUTHERFORD HILL WINERY is housed in a stunning building of weathered redwood in the shape of a chalet-barn, draped with virginia creeper and wisteria and bounded by grass and flowers. The winery crowns a plateau and enjoys the same spectacular valley views that you pay a high price to enjoy at the neighboring Auberge du Soleil. Paths lead down the hillside to picnic tables set under olive trees where the views will tempt you to wile away an afternoon. Guides at Rutherford Hill are friendly and quite proud of (as well as knowledgeable about) the winery. Although winemaking procedures are basically the same regardless of a winery's production, Rutherford Hill is a small winery and the guide's explanation of the step-by-step process seems easier to understand than the same explanation at a winery on a much grander scale. Visitors are encouraged to ask questions. Advance reservations are not needed, but for more information call (707) 963-1871.

Rutherford Hill is the dream of a number of independent vintners who together purchased what was once the Souverain Winery (now located in the Sonoma Valley) in order to process and control the production of their limited quantities of grapes into wine. Labels depict which vineyard is responsible for any given bottle of wine. It is a centuries-old European tradition that great wines carry the names of the individual vineyards from which they are made. The owners also constructed the largest expanse of underground caves in the valley - these maintain a constant natural temperature of 58 degrees which minimizes evaporation far more successfully than when temperatures are controlled by air conditioning. The tour of Rutherford Hill includes a visit to these caves which are impressive but stark as a result of their newness and the recent vintages that they guard. The tour of Rutherford Hill both begins and ends in its dramatic reception and tasting hall. Rutherford is also the California capital for petanque, an ancient Mediterranean game of bowls, and in addition to its winery, picnic grounds and spectacular views also affords guests the opportunity to play on its petanque courts.

From Rutherford Hill Winery return to the Silverado Trail and travel north approximately 4 miles to what is Pope Street on your left and Howell Mountain Road on your right. Take Howell Mountain Road and then take the first left to the entrance of MEADOWOOD RESORT HOTEL, a spectacular property, offering a host of facilities to enhance your wine-tasting itinerary - golf, tennis, croquet, swimming pools, walks and fine restaurants. Meadowood's country-style lodges are so discreetly positioned throughout its 256-acre estate that you enjoy all the amenities of a resort without feeling part of one.

Meadowood Resort Hotel
St Helena

DESTINATION II CALISTOGA

Leaving Meadowood, cross the Silverado Trail onto Pope Street which takes a scenic back route to the south end of ST HELENA. Turn north (right) onto highway 29 which takes you down this lovely town's Main Street lined with elegant stores, boutiques and restaurants. Detour east two blocks off Main Street via Adams Street to ST HELENA'S LIBRARY AND MUSEUM. The library has a very interesting section on wine and one wing of the museum is dedicated to Robert Louis Stevenson, the great Scotsman who settled with his new bride in an old miner's shack northeast of Calistoga. It was here that he wrote *Silverado Squatters*, a book romantically promoting the beauty of the Napa Valley.

(Stevenson buffs can also visit the ROBERT LOUIS STEVENSON PARK on highway 29 between Calistoga and Middletown and you can also make an appointment to tour Schramsburg Vineyards, the winery Stevenson featured in his chronicles of the wine country. SCHRAMSBERG VINEYARDS which offers tours at 10.00AM and 2.00PM by appointment, (707) 942-4558, is tucked in the western foothills just off highway 29 to the south of Calistoga. The production of sparkling wine dominates the several tunnels and cellar. Quantities are so limited that tasting is not possible, but, as the proprietors remark, visitors to Schramsberg Vineyards are usually already familiar with the excellence of their wines.)

As highway 29 leaves the commercial district of St Helena and enters a very exclusive residential district on its northern borders, watch carefully for the gated entry to BERINGER VINEYARDS, set on knoll, surrounded by beautifully landscaped grounds of mature trees, lawns and gardens. What was once the home of the founding Beringer family now houses a wine and gift shop. Reflecting its heritage and standing as a tribute to one of the valley's founding wineries, the dramatic stone and half-timbered building with a slate roof was one of two family homes built as a replica of the German home that Frederick and his brother Jacob left behind when they emigrated. The second and smaller home is currently under restoration. Half-hour tours are offered daily and their availability and times are posted outside the original old cellar. Tours emphasize the historical aspect of the winery and include a memorable visit through the tunnels and caverns where the wine is aged in barrels. Advance reservations for tours, which leave on the hour and half-hour, are not needed: (707) 963-7115.

From Beringer head north another 4 miles and then turn right on Larkmead Lane. The HANNS KORNELL WINERY, a name synonymous with fine champagne is located on Larkmead Lane. Hanns Kornell is devoted entirely to the production of traditional, bottle-fermented sparkling wines. Visitors are welcome and tours are informal and personalized to suit the group and the production activities of any particular day or hour (707) 963-1237. The tour is more informative than visual: an in-depth, detailed explanation is offered about the traditional methods of making sparkling wine. Kornell is family owned, and the owner, Hanns Kornell, is often about, working there as he has been every day for the past 35 years.

A large posted sign on highway 29 instructs you to turn just a few miles farther at Dunaweal Lane to visit STERLING VINEYARDS. Reminiscent of a Moorish castle, Sterling Vineyards enjoys a crowning position on a hill idyllically set in the middle of the valley. From the winery you can savor panoramic views looking down through tall pines to a checkerboard of vineyards. Access to Sterling is possible only by small gondolas: for a fee of $5.00 you can ride the aerial tramway from parking lot to winery and back. Arrows and detailed signs direct you on an informative but impersonal, self-guided tour through the maze of rooms that comprise the winery. By appointment a special guided tour is offered at 11:00AM and 2:00PM Monday through Friday (707) 942-5151. The last flight of steps leads up to the tasting room from which the views are a bit disappointing. One explanation offered as to why they didn't take advantage of the possible 360-degree views was that, if offered, no one would move on - and it is probably true! Although limited, the views are lovely, as is the wine. Another subtle but equally unique and inviting feature about Sterling is the wonderful melodic sound of bells that ring out every quarter hour, they once hung in London's St Dunstan's-in-the-East Church.

The delightful town of CALISTOGA is just a few miles north from Sterling Vineyards at the intersection of highway 29 and highway 128. Bounded by rugged foothills and vineyards, Calistoga is an attractive town servicing local residents and tourists alike. Its main street, Lincoln Avenue, is lined on both sides by attractive shops and numerous restaurants. This charming town has been famous ever since Spanish explorers arrived in 1823 and observed Indians taking mud baths in steamy marshes. Sam Brannan, who purchased a square mile of land at the foot of Mount St Helena, gave the town its name: he wanted the place to be the "Saratoga of California" and so called it Calistoga. He bought the land in the early 1860s and by 1866 was ready to open his resort of a few cottages and palm trees. The oldest surviving railroad depot in California, now serving as a quaint and historic shopping mall, received its first trainload of passengers when they came to Calistoga for the much-publicized opening of Sam Brannan's resort. For more than one hundred years, Calistoga has attracted visitors from all over the world, primarily for its hot springs and spas. People came in search of its glorious, healing waters long before the region became a popular destination for its wineries.

There are many spa facilities to choose from - on the eastern end of town look for the Calistoga Spa and Hot Springs (1006 Washington Street, Calistoga 94515, (707) 942-6269). Their facilities are newly renovated, expansive and modern and the attendants are professional and very nice. Offered are volcanic ash mud baths, mineral baths, steam baths, blanket wraps and massage. The entire package, "the works", takes almost two hours and their rates are very competitive.

If you are feeling adventurous, visit the Calistoga Soaring Center (1546 Lincoln Avenue, Calistoga 94515, (707) 942-5592) and arrange for a glider ride. You can also take a balloon flight with Once in a Lifetime (P.O. Box 795, Calistoga 94515, (707) 942-6541). A sunrise launch is arranged from a selection of wineries. This one-hour fantasy voyage includes a gourmet brunch at the Mount View Hotel.

If you have never seen a geyser, travel a few miles farther north from Calistoga on highway 128 in the direction of Lakeport to Tubbs Lane. Turn right onto Tubbs Lane and in a 1/2 mile you see the entrance to the OLD FAITHFUL GEYSER on the left. Anticipated at intervals of every 50 minutes, Old Faithful erupts with a spume of about 4,000 gallons of water reaching more than 60 feet into the air. Old Faithful is said to be one of only three such regularly erupting geysers in the world. Although the staging is a bit honky-tonk, the geyser is an interesting natural phenomenon.

Your home for tonight, MEADOWLARK COUNTRY HOUSE & INN, is located just a short distance north of Calistoga on Petrified Forest Road. Although the inn appears new it actually dates back to 1886. This is one of those inns that gives guests the feeling that they have their own wine country home to return to. Take a walk through the 20 acres of wooded grounds, or wander down to the pasture to see the Arabian horses, or simply spend a quiet afternoon poolside. Your host, Kurt Stevens, sets an air of informality matched with European hospitality.

Meadowlark Country House & Inn
Calistoga

DESTINATION III — GLEN ELLEN

Leaving Meadowlark, take the Petrified Forest Road in the direction of Santa Rosa foresaking the Napa for the neighboring Sonoma wine valley. The road climbs and winds a scenic 10 miles through forest and past pastures where cattle graze next to neighboring vineyards and orchards of apples and almonds. You may wish to stop at the rather commercial California Petrified Forest, a grove of redwoods which was petrified by ash from the volcanic eruption of Mount St Helena over 6 million years ago. It is this same ash that is responsible for fertile wine valley soils.

On the residential outskirts of SANTA ROSA Petrified Forest Road merges with highway 12 and you turn south (left) towards Sonoma. This highway travels down the center of Sonoma Valley, often referred to as the "Valley of the Moon" after Jack London's famous novel of the same name. London fell in love with Sonoma Valley's magnificent landscape - a wondrous mix of high hills, oak-covered knolls, open pastures, forests of oaks, madrones, fir and redwood trees, grassy fields and streams. The author chose the valley as his home - a "quiet place in the country to write and loaf in and get out of Nature that something which we all need, only most of us don't know it."

Your first destination in this lovely valley, CHATEAU ST JEAN, lies about 7 miles south of Santa Rosa on the left, on highway 12. An extremely pretty road winds up through the vineyards to the strikingly beautiful winery and main house surrounded by lush lawns. With the exception of its mock tower, Chateau St Jean is Mediterranean French in its architecture; its red tile roofs and arched entries stunning against a backdrop of green hills. The estate is dedicated exclusively to the production of premium wines, but as a visitor you will feel that the winery's chief concern is making visitors feel welcome by outlining a very comprehensive self-guided tour of the winemaking process. After the tour you cross the courtyard to the original "chateau" for complimentary tasting. Any questions you might have will be answered graciously. For further information call (707) 833-4134.

Your next winery, Kenwood, is next door and completely different in character. KENWOOD VINEYARDS occupies an attractive complex of old wooden barns where wine is produced, stored and tasted. Tours of this small winery are offered by appointment (707) 833-5891. Ask the friendly staff at the tasting room if you can sample their Beltane Chardonnay for it is produced from grapes grown at Beltane Ranch, your destination for tonight.

BELTANE RANCH is well signposted on your left just a few miles south of Kenwood. The ranch's principal building is a pale yellow clapboard house, encircled by broad verandahs on each of its two stories and surrounded by a short, white picket fence. Fronted by vineyards and backed by oak trees, the ranch-house has a lovely setting. Your innkeeper Rosemary Wood offers bed and breakfast accommodation to guests in her lovely old home. The house has no internal staircase, so each room has a private entrance off the verandah - which was probably a very handy arrangement when this was the weekend retreat of a San Francisco madame. Incidentally, this also explains the rather southern architecture of the house as "madame" hailed from Louisiana. Arrive early as Beltane Ranch is reason enough to visit the Sonoma Valley. This is such a peaceful spot that you may be tempted to abandon the rest of the valley's sightseeing.

Beltane Ranch
Glen Ellen

GLEN ELLEN, a quiet little country town set in a wooded valley, lies just a few miles south of Beltane Ranch. Follow the main road through town, following signs for Jack London State Park. Before you reach the park take time to visit the GLEN ELLEN WINERY, a family-run winery in the truest sense of the word - signs warn to watch for children at play. From babies to Goober, the family dog and "official reception committee", everyone at Glen Ellen is warm and friendly. If it's close to lunch time, take advantage of picnic tables set under redwood trees. The tasting room is quite a hike from the parking lot, so if someone in your party has difficulty with a hilly driveway, continue on to the handicapped area, or circle round to drop them in the front. The Benziger family were wine importers in New York and moved here less than ten years ago to produce their own wines. They have concentrated successfully on marketing their moderately priced wines to large outlets and consequently most Californians are familiar with their wine. No official tours are offered, but you are welcome to tour the property on your own (707) 996-1066.

Nearby JACK LONDON STATE PARK, where Jack London is buried, is a lovely wooded park established as a tribute to the famous author who has had such an impact on the Sonoma Valley. This strikingly handsome man lived a life of rugged adventure and wrote passionately about life's struggles and how to survive them with integrity. In the 16 years prior to his death at age 40, he wrote 50 novels that were immensely popular and are today considered classics. Two of his more renowned novels are *Call of the Wild* and *The Sea Wolf.* This park offers a fitting tribute to Jack London, a courageous, dynamic man, full of life and concern for his fellows. For further information call (707) 938-5216.

In the park you can visit the ruins of Wolf House (London's dream house which mysteriously burned to the ground the night of its completion), Beauty Cottage (the cottage where London wrote much of his later work) and The House of Happy Walls (the home that Charmian London built after her husband's death). The House of Happy Walls is now an interesting museum that depicts London's life through numerous photographs, writings and furnishings that belonged to the author. From the museum walks lead to the other homes and the gravesite.

From the park return to Arnold Drive and travel south (past the Sonoma State Home) to Madrone where you turn left, crossing over to highway 12 that takes you into the heart of Sonoma.

SONOMA is a gem of a town. By simply exploring the boundaries of its main square you will glimpse some of California's most important periods in history. (A small admission price is charged to tour Sonoma's historic buildings.) On the square's northern edge sits the SONOMA BARRACKS, a two-story, adobe building which was the Mexican Provincial headquarters for the Northern Frontier under the command of Mariano Guadalupe Vallejo. The adjacent wood-frame TOSCANO HOTEL has been restored and on weekends docents provide interesting tours through the rooms. The nearby MISSION SAN FRANCISCO SOLANO DE SONOMA, the last Franciscan mission built in California, was restored in the early 1900s. If you visit during the week you may see elementary-school children, dressed as missionaries with their simple cloaks and rope ties, experiencing history "hands on" as they work with crafts and tools from the days of the missionaries. In one hall of the mission is an unusually beautiful collection of watercolor paintings of many of California's missions. The long, low adobe building across the way, THE BLUE WIG INN, originally built to house soldiers assigned to the mission, enjoyed a more colorful existence as a saloon and gambling room during the gold rush days.

In addition to the historic sites on Sonoma's plaza, there are numerous shops and boutiques to investigate. There are also some wonderful specialty food stores where you can purchase picnic supplies. The Sonoma Cheese Factory on Spain Street is interesting to visit and easy to pop into between historic sites. The front of the shop has a deli and at back, behind a glass partition, you can observe the making of cheese. On East Street, you can purchase delicious bread at the Sonoma French Bread shop and enjoy a tasty ice cream at the ice cream parlor.

Leaving the square, go east on Napa Boulevard for 2 miles to Old Winery Road where you turn left to the BUENA VISTA WINERY, the region's oldest winery. Nestled in a wooded glen, the old stone, ivy-covered buildings are very picturesque with arched caverns and old stone walls making the atmosphere particularly inviting. Picnic tables are set under the trees (it is hard to find a lunch spot in summer months). Wine tasting is offered in the old press house and a self-guided tour directs you through the old stone barn and three tunnels.

Mission San Francisco Solano - Sonoma

General Vallejo, the Military Commander and Director of Colonization of the Northern Frontier (until the Bear Flag Revolution established California as a free and independent republic) lived nearby with his wife and 12 children. VALLEJO'S HOME, "Lachryma Montis" (translated to mean mountain tear, an adaptation of the Indian name given to a free-flowing spring that surrounds the property) is well signposted on the outskirts of town on Spain Street. In its day this lovely Victorian-style home was considered one of the most elegant and lavishly decorated homes in the area, and is still attractively furnished.

After you leave the Sonoma Valley, one more winery awaits you as you return to San Francisco. When highway 12 deadends at highway 116, turn right onto highway 116 (signposted Petaluma) and at the intersection of highway 121 turn left in the direction of San Francisco. A short drive brings you to the GLORIA FERRER WINERY, a fitting grand finale for this wine country itinerary. The Ferrer family hail from Catalonia in Spain and have only recently brought their expertise on Spanish sparkling wines to the Sonoma Valley. Consequently, the handsome winery with its stucco walls and tiled roof resembles a small Catalonian village. A wide road sweeps up to the winery through newly planted vineyards. As the vineyards have yet to mature, the Ferrer family currently contracts for local grapes to produce their sparkling wines. Very informative and interesting tours start from the tasting room, a large, spacious room whose windows look out over the vineyards and valley. Most of the narrative is given in a room decorated with winemaking instruments used a half a century ago in the Ferrers' winery in Spain. The riddling of the bottles to capture the sediment is explained, and then you go to the observation room to see the process of freezing then disgorging the sediment, corking, cleaning and labeling the bottles of sparkling wine. The tour then descends into a maze of interconnected wine storage tunnels: while the winery has not reached its capacity in terms of production, it is awesome to stand next to towering heights of stacked bottles. The tour concludes back in the tasting room. A fee is charged to sample the sparkling wine, but "tapas", Spanish hors d'oeuvres, are complimentary. For further information call (707) 996-7256.

From Gloria Ferrer it is about an hour's drive back to San Francisco by continuing along highway 121 to highway 37 and onto highway 101 which takes you over the Golden Gate Bridge into San Francisco.

NOTE: We have tried to be as accurate as possible when giving information about touring wineries but things change, so be certain to give each winery a call in advance to see whether or not they are open and whether you need an appointment.

WEATHER WISE: The Napa and Sonoma Valleys have a very similar climate. Summer days can be scorching hot and the valleys' roads are often clogged with visitors. Fall gives way to mild, sunny days, cooler afternoons and crisp evenings. From fall through spring you can expect rain. In winter temperatures are several degrees cooler than in the nearby San Francisco Bay Area.

Places to Stay in California

The location of the Albion River Inn is splendid, right on the bluff overlooking the handsome bay formed by the mouth of the Albion River as it flows into the ocean. Although this is a newly built hotel, the architecture creates the ambiance of a New England village: softly-hued clusters of cottages perch on the cliffs surrounded by a meadow where long grass waves in the wind. Gardens filled with brightly colored flowers line the walkways along the bluff and the quiet is broken only by the deep-throated call of the fog horn. Each of the bedrooms offers a sweeping view of the inlet where the fishing boats bob about in the ever-changing tides. All of the rooms are spacious, romantic and very private - many even have wood-burning fireplaces. The decor is most attractive and, although not antique, reflects the hand of a professional decorator. There is an excellent restaurant adjacent to the inn with picture windows overlooking the sea - it is a good idea to request dinner reservations when booking your room. Every morning in the reception lounge a Continental breakfast is served which guests can take on trays to their room. Also coffee makers are set up in each room so guests can enjoy hot drinks whenever they want. *Directions:* From San Francisco drive north on highway 101 to Cloverdale, west on highway 128 to highway 1 and north to Albion. The Albion River Inn is on the northwest side of the Albion Bridge.

ALBION RIVER INN
Innkeepers: Peter Wells & Flurry Healy
Albion, CA 95410
Tel: (707) 937-1919
20 bedrooms with private bathrooms
Double from $80 to $175
Open: all year
Credit cards: MC, VS
Children accepted

Aptos, just two hours south of San Francisco, is best known as a beach resort. Most tourists never realize that tucked into the coastal hills are beautiful redwood glens and, best yet, adjacent to the redwood forest is Mangels House, an elegant, large, redwood home, painted white and enwrapped with a two-tiered verandah. Once the holiday home of the wealthy Mangels family, who made their fortune in the sugar beet industry, Mangels House now belongs to Jacqueline and Ron Fisher. You enter into a large living room dominated by a tall stone fireplace which is surrounded by two comfortable floral-patterned sofas and an easy chair. To the left is a formal dining room where a full breakfast is served every morning. The five individually decorated bedrooms vary considerably in size. Four rooms have a traditional ambiance while the other has an African motif, a reflection of the years that the Fisher family lived in Africa. One of the nicest aspects of Mangels House is its woodland location just a five-minute drive from the beach. *Directions:* From Santa Cruz, drive 6 miles south on highway 101, taking the Seacliff Beach-Aptos exit over the freeway (away from the bay). Turn right at the traffic lights onto Soquel Drive. Just before the Aptos Station Shopping Center turn left onto Aptos Creek Road. The house is in the woods 1/2 mile on your right.

MANGELS HOUSE
Innkeeper: Jacqueline Fisher
570 Aptos Creek Road
Aptos, CA 95001
Tel: (408) 688-7982
5 bedrooms, 3 with private bathrooms
Double from $88 to $110
Open: all year except Christmas
Credit cards: MC, VS
Children accepted over 12

A lush green lawn shaded by towering pines fronts the Gold Mountain Manor. Built to provide luxurious accommodations for the elite, the Manor has also served as a brothel and family residence before it recently once again became an exclusive inn. The decor of this mountain log cabin is so cozy and inviting that it is often used as a backdrop for magazine layouts and advertisements - the central parlor whose walls are hung with prints has a dramatic stone fireplace fronted by inviting, well-worn chairs. The seven bedrooms have different decor and original stencil patterns dress a number of walls to blend with or set a theme. At the top of the stairs the Wildcat Room, small but cozy, is the only room without a private fireplace. The Lucky Baldwin Room is handsomely decorated with plaids and tartan robes are laid out for guests' use. The Clark Gable Room commemorates the time this famous actor brought his love, Carole Lombard, for a romantic retreat: the fireplace is from his mountain cabin in Fawnskin. While the manor is ready for a new coat of paint and some refurbishments, it is a cozy and rustic retreat. *Directions:* From Los Angeles take I-10 to San Bernardino, then highway 215 north to 30 east until it ends. Follow Big Bear signs to highway 330 and go 33 miles to Big Bear Dam where you take North Shore Drive to Fawnskin. Turn left on Anita 7 miles past Fawnskin.

GOLD MOUNTAIN MANOR
Innkeeper: Trish Hastings
1117 Anita, P.O. Box 2027
Big Bear City, CA 92314
Tel: (714) 585-6997
7 bedrooms, 3 with private bathrooms
Double from $70 to $135
Open: all year
Credit cards: none accepted
Children accepted over 12

There is no coastline in the world more dramatically splendid than Big Sur, a rugged, rocky stretch along the Pacific Ocean where steep hills plunge into the sea to greet the determined, crashing surf. Happily for the traveller, the Ventana is nestled back in the hills, surrounded by 240 acres of meadows and forests, complementing the beauty of Big Sur. However, in contrast to the coastline, there is nothing rugged about Ventana. It pretends to be somewhat rustic, but in reality, behind the weathered wooden facade of the cottages, lies a most sophisticated, deluxe resort where guests are pampered and provided with every luxury. The Ventana has grown in stages, so each cluster of natural wood buildings has its own patina of age. The outsides are not especially attractive, but, inside, each guest room is spacious and decorator-perfect. The decor varies (depending upon which section you are in) but each guest room has the same country ambiance with natural wood panelling, luxurious fabrics and wicker chairs. Most rooms have a large terrace with a latticed wood screen. All have a pretty view either of the hills and forest or to the sea on the far horizon. There are two lounges where beverages are served in the afternoon and breakfast (a scrumptious buffet of home-baked pastries and fruit) is set out each morning. Guests can either take a tray to their room, or eat on one of the tables in the lounge or outside on the terrace. *Directions:* 28 miles south of Carmel on highway 1.

VENTANA
Innkeeper: Robert Bussinger
Big Sur, CA 93920
Tel: (408) 667-2331
60 bedrooms with private bathrooms
Double from $145 to $350
Open: all year
Credit cards: all major
Inappropriate for children

The Elms Bed & Breakfast was built in 1871 and is on the National Register of Historic Places. Diane Harris and Marc Cathey have restored this handsome and romantic two-story home set behind a wrought-iron fence in a garden, next to a lovely park. In general, the decor is ornate, in keeping with the style of the house. Marc and Diane have been both creative and clever in selecting a theme for each of the bedrooms. A steep staircase winds up to the Judge Palmer Room, dramatic with a four-poster bed, marble fireplace and private balcony, and the Bordello Room, whimsical with many hats, a feather boa and a neon sign decorating the walls. On the third floor the Katherine Hepburn Room with a brass bed and wicker furniture looks out at the mountains through a French window and the Sam Brannan Room oozes coziness with its twin brass beds and a dormer window seat. On each floor, both rooms share a large bath with shower. Wine and cheese are offered afternoons in the decorative salon. Tea and coffee are served in your room in the morning and a gourmet breakfast is set in the elegant dining room. Diane and Marc bustle about tending to their guests with much care. *Directions:* Follow highway 29 as it winds to the right into Calistoga, and before reaching the heart of downtown, turn left on Cedar Street. The Elms is on your right.

THE ELMS BED & BREAKFAST
Innkeepers: Diane Harris & Marc Cathey
1300 Cedar Street
Calistoga, CA 94515
Tel: (707) 942-9476
4 bedrooms, each 2 rooms share a bath
Double from $85 to $95
Open: all year
Credit cards: none accepted
Inappropriate for children

To the north of Calistoga, just a driveway's distance off highway 128, a remodeled turn-of-the-century farmhouse has been converted to Foothill House bed and breakfast. Each of the three suites has been decorated around a colorful handmade quilt and furnished attractively - a woodburning stove or fireplace and refrigerator for picnic supplies are welcome extras. The Evergreen Suite is a large room with an additional alcove bed, jacuzzi whirlpool tub and a private deck. The Foothill Lupine Suite is a long room that fronts the driveway and has a bed at one end and a wood-burning stove, sitting area with loveseat at the other. The Redwood Room is decorated in rusts and blues and opens onto the back garden. The Sun Room serves as a central area for guests: hot beverages are always available and in the evening guests gather for "wine appreciation hour". While you are out at dinner your bed is turned down, fresh towels are placed in the bathroom, a decanter of sherry is set out, homemade "Sweet Dream" cookies are left bedside in a miniature cookie jar with a personal note, the lights are dimmed and classical music sets a romantic mood for your return. *Directions:* From Calistoga, travel north on Foothill Boulevard (highway 128) 1 1/2 miles to Foothill House on your left.

FOOTHILL HOUSE
Innkeepers: Susan & Michael Clow
3037 Foothill Boulevard
Calistoga, CA 94515
Tel: (707) 942-6933
3 suites with private bathrooms
Double from $75 to $105
Open: all year
Credit cards: MC, VS
Children accepted over 12

With the Hanns Kornell Winery as its neighbor, the Larkmead Country Inn is tucked a short distance off the St Helena Highway on Larkmead Lane. Set behind a fieldstone fence and gates, this lovely two-story, white clapboard home was built by one of the first wine producing families in the Napa Valley. Its broad porches shaded by magnificent sycamores, magnolias and cypress trees provide a lovely place to settle after a day of wine tasting. The entrance to the inn is at back and up a flight of stairs to the second floor. Owned and managed by Gene and Joan Garbarino, the inn is beautifully furnished with antiques, lovely paintings and prints and Persian carpets. Guests are encouraged to enjoy the warm ambiance of the central living room with a large fireplace, bay window and upstairs porch. The four guest rooms are named after wines of the Napa Valley and appropriately look out over the surrounding vineyards. Chardonnay and Chablis are twin-bedded rooms while Chenin Blanc and Beaujolais are furnished with queen beds. Each room is attractively furnished, is air-conditioned and has a private bath or shower. Chablis and Beaujolais enjoy the privacy of an enclosed porch. *Directions:* Located 4 1/2 miles north of St Helena off highway 29 on Larkmead Lane. Look for the home on the right just before the Hanns Kornell Winery - there is no sign advertising the inn.

LARKMEAD COUNTRY INN
Innkeeper: Joan Garbarino
1103 Larkmead Lane
Calistoga, CA 94515
Tel: (707) 942-5360
4 bedrooms with private bathrooms
Double from $88 to $95
Closed: December & January
Credit cards: none accepted
Inappropriate for children

Meadowlark Country House & Inn is located at the northernmost end of the Napa Valley, buffered from any road noise by a long drive and 20 acres of grounds that contain a large swimming pool, a pasture grazed by magnificent Arabian horses and woodland walks that wind beneath cherry trees. The two-story home appears new, but was originally built in 1886. Inside, light wood floors contrast beautifully with English country-pine antiques and handsome fabrics. The atmosphere is one of sophisticated elegance and the hospitality is described as "European". It is a country house where guests can relax and make themselves "at home". The spacious living room with its large French windows, the country-French dining room and large verandah are all for guests' use. Kurt sets guests at ease and wants them to enjoy the inn as if it were their home in the country. Meadowlark opened in the spring of 1988 and its guest register reflects numerous repeat visitors. One guest who reserved a room confusing the inn with the Meadowood Resort, claims it is the "best mistake she ever made!" *Directions:* Take Foothill Boulevard north from Calistoga to Petrified Forest Road. The road will be posted with signs to San Francisco and Santa Rosa. Meadowlark is on the left just a few hundred yards off Foothill Boulevard.

MEADOWLARK COUNTRY HOUSE & INN
Innkeeper: Kurt Stevens
601 Petrified Forest Road
Calistoga, CA 94515
Tel: (707) 942-5651
4 bedrooms with private bathrooms
Double from $95 to $125
Open: all year
Credit cards: none accepted
Children accepted over 12

The Mount View Hotel makes a refreshing change from the albeit charming but numerous country and Victorian inns. Completely renovated in 1980, the Mount View Hotel's furnishings and decor have been selected to capture the mood of Europe in the 1930s. The lobby is comfortable and airy, furnished with overstuffed sofas and chrome chairs with a large fireplace and bountiful arrangements of flowers. The restaurant is attractively staged with caned-back chairs, framed advertisements of the '30s and walls painted an attractive light plum. Fender's Lounge is a fun and inviting bar where live music fills the air each night. The bedrooms are individually decorated, named after personalities of the '30s and '40s and have either double, queen or twin beds. Turndown service and a full American breakfast are included in the reasonable room rates. The Mount View Hotel is considered an art deco landmark and features on the National Register of Historic Places. A swimming pool provides a welcome respite on a hot summer day. The hotel prides itself on its friendly staff who make you feel both welcome and appreciated. Built in 1917 on the site of the European Hotel, the hotel was one of the first full-service hotels in the Napa Valley and has catered for years to an international clientele in search of the healing Calistoga hot springs and mud baths. *Directions:* The hotel is on Lincoln Avenue, the main street of Calistoga.

MOUNT VIEW HOTEL
Manager: Terry Batley
1457 Lincoln Avenue
Calistoga, CA 94515
Tel: (707) 942-6877
34 bedrooms with private bathrooms
Double from $50 to $110
Open: all year
Credit cards: all major
Children accepted

Built to resemble a log cabin, The J. Patrick House, lovingly named for Molly's father, John Patrick Lynch, is a newly constructed inn where great care has been taken to establish an old-world ambiance. The living room is especially inviting, its open log fire surrounded by comfy sofa and chairs and country knickknacks. A breakfast of fresh fruit, muffins, bread, hot beverages and fresh squeezed orange juice is served in a cheerful nook off the cozy living room which overlooks a small but lovely garden. One bedroom is in the main house while the remainder are in an annex across the back garden. Named for counties in Ireland: Galway, Dublin, Tipperary, Kerry, Limerick, Donegal and Kilkenny, each room has a fireplace (one has a woodburning stove) and window seat and was individually decorated by Molly. All the rooms have bath and shower except one which has only a shower. The back bedrooms enjoy a lovely little sitting room where guests are surprised with milk and cookies at night. Before departing you can clean your windscreen using the Windex and towels hung in the parking area. Also, be sure to take one of the sprigs of lavender hung outside above the porch: they add a lovely scent to the air and are a wonderful keepsake. *Directions:* From highway 1 turn east, into Cambria, on Burton Drive.

THE J. PATRICK HOUSE
Innkeeper: Molly Lynch
2990 Burton Drive
Cambria, CA 93428
Tel: (805) 927-3812
8 bedrooms with private bathrooms
Doubles $95
Open: all year
Credit cards: MC, VS
Children accepted over 15

The Olallieberry Inn was built in 1872 and features on the National Register of Historic Buildings. It is a darling, simple country clapboard cottage that has been a bed and breakfast for a good many years. Management is especially friendly and someone is always about to welcome you to the inn. A guest book is left in every room and each is filled with telling praises. The inn has six bedrooms, three upstairs and three downstairs. They are all with private bath, but not all bathrooms are en suite - if a bathroom is located down the hall from a room, a small blackboard directs you to its location. The bedroom decor is very romantic, fussy Victorian, with lots of lace and feminine touches. The country kitchen set with one long antique trestle table, is delightful, looking out onto the greenery of the back yard with a rather ornate fountain, lawn and creek. Guests breakfast here on a hearty Continental breakfast of mixed fruits and berries, yoghurt, granola, hot quiche, croissants and rolls served with olallieberry jam. Complimentary refreshments are served between 5:00 and 6:00 PM. *Directions:* The Olallieberry Inn is on Cambria's Main Street just a few blocks south of East Village.

OLALLIEBERRY INN
Innkeeper: Linda Boyers
2476 Main Street
Cambria, CA 93428
Tel: (805) 927-3222
6 bedrooms with private bathrooms
Double from $75 to $90
Open: all year
Credit cards: MC, VS
Children accepted over 13

The Cobblestone Inn is a remarkable conversion of a rather ordinary motel into a country inn with great appeal: the central parking courtyard has been paved and enhanced with trees, flowers and creepers, a brick patio has been set with tables and chairs and the inn has been exquisitely decorated and furnished in an appealing country-American style. The Cobblestone Inn is part of a group of small hotels that pride themselves on having perfected the art of personalized innkeeping. This one is certainly no exception. The staff are young, enthusiastic and attentive and you feel thoroughly spoiled by all the little extras: flowers, fruit, balloons announcing special occasions, a handwritten note welcoming you by name, your bed turned down at night and a newspaper at your door in the morning. Besides their delightful decor, bedrooms have every amenity: good reading lights, refrigerator, phone, television and fireplace. Beverages and snacks are always available. Hearty hors d'oeuvres arrive in the evening. A full buffet breakfast is served and you can take it outside to the patio to enjoy the sunshine of a Carmel morning. With all this comfort and attention it is not surprising that reservations need to be made well in advance. *Directions:* From highway 1 take the Ocean Avenue exit, then turn left on Junipero. The Cobblestone is on your right on the corner of 8th Street.

COBBLESTONE INN
Innkeeper: Aileen Kelly
P.O. Box 3185, Corner of Junipero & 8th Streets
Carmel, CA 93921
Tel: (408) 625-5222
24 bedrooms with private bathrooms
Double from $90 to $170
Open: all year
Credit cards: all major
Children accepted

In a quiet district of Carmel within easy walking distance of Ocean Avenue (the principal shopping street) stands The Happy Landing, a group of bright pink colorwashed cottages, accented by vivid teal blue paintwork. The cottages are clustered around beautiful gardens banked high with colorful flowers. Pots and baskets of flowers fill every nook and cranny. This picture-perfect garden contains an array of whimsical garden statuary, such as a gnome fishing in the pond, a frog fountain and several large metal birds. Arched cottage doors lead into the bedrooms where high cathedral ceilings give a spacious feeling. The rooms appear a bit dated, though pleasantly furnished; some have fireplaces and sitting rooms and all have spotless older-style bathrooms. Everything throughout the inn is immaculately tended. A fun touch: when you open your curtains in the morning it is the signal that you would like your breakfast tray brought to you. Many guests enjoy breakfast in the pretty garden amongst the flowers. Guests are welcome to use the distinctive, large, cathedral-ceilinged reception/common room where teas and coffee are provided in the afternoon. *Directions:* Take the Ocean Avenue exit from highway 1 to Monte Verde where you turn right. The Happy Landing is on your right between 5th and 6th Streets.

THE HAPPY LANDING
Innkeepers: Carl & Jeannine George
Monte Verde, P.O. Box 2619
Carmel, CA 93921
Tel: (408) 624-7917
7 bedrooms with private bathrooms
Double from $80 to $135
Open: all year
Credit cards: MC, VS
Children accepted over 12

With the ocean three blocks away, Sea View Inn is within easy walking distance of the much photographed Carmel beach and it may just be possible to catch the tiniest glimpse of the ocean through the trees from the third floor of the inn. This large Victorian house looks as though it were once a large home, when in fact it has always been an inn. Cream-colored board and batten wainscoting accented by a plate rail displaying antiques and interesting bric-a-brac sets the welcoming mood for the living room and adjacent parlor - both rooms are warmed by cozy fireplaces. Games, books and magazines add a comfortable, lived-in feel. The largest bedrooms are found on the second floor. Room 6 is most attractive in shades of white on white complemented by pine furniture. The adjacent room 7 has stark white walls and window blinds with a dramatic Oriental-style four-poster bed draped with blue and white Chinese motif fabric. The four tiny bedrooms on the third floor provide the snuggest of accommodation tucked under the steeply slanting attic ceilings. Each is lavishly decorated in a mellow English floral print gathered into canopies and covering huge bed pillows. *Directions:* Take the Ocean Avenue exit from highway 1 to Camino Real where you turn left - Sea View Inn is just after 11th Street.

SEA VIEW INN
Innkeepers: Marshall & Diane Hydorn
P.O. Box 4138
Camino Real between 11th & 12th Streets
Carmel, CA 93921
Tel: (408) 624-8778
8 bedrooms, 6 with private bathrooms
Double from $70 to $100
Open: all year
Credit cards: MC, VS
Children accepted over 12

Sundial Lodge has a perfect location in Carmel, being just a few short steps from the main shopping streets and within walking distance of her white sand beach. The central red-brick, flower-filled courtyard is the focal point of the lodge, a lush oasis of gaily colored bushes, hanging baskets, flowers and ferns. Overlooking the courtyard, the spacious, airy bedrooms have a Victorian or French country theme, all being freshly decorated and pleasantly furnished with reproduction furniture. Each room is well equipped with good reading lights, a phone and television - several rooms have small kitchens. Continental breakfast is served buffet-style in the reception room. It is most pleasant to fix a tray of juices, muffins and coffee and repair to the sunny patio. And on misty days there is no nicer way to start the day than breakfast by the fireside. Parking is always a problem in Carmel and because the lodge does not have guest parking you must hunt for nearby unmetered street parking. *Directions:* Take the Ocean Avenue exit from highway 1 to Monte Verde where you turn left - Sundial Lodge is next to City Hall before you come to 7th Ave.

SUNDIAL LODGE
Innkeeper: Milton Higgins
P.O. Box J
Monte Verde at Seventh Street
Carmel, CA 93921
Tel: (408) 624-8578
19 bedrooms with private bathrooms
Double from $90 to $150
Open: all year
Credit cards: MC, VS
Children accepted over 12

Carmel's quaint gingerbread architecture, profusion of colorful flowers and tall, shady trees is mimicked by the Vagabond's House Inn. Set around a flagstone courtyard shaded by a giant oak tree and surrounded by fuchsias, azaleas, camelias and rhododendrons, the buildings are storybook English cottage, brick and half-timbered topped by a thick shake roof, making this one of Carmel's most atmospheric places to stay. Each of the guest rooms opens onto the courtyard and many have cozy fireplaces and sitting nooks. In the morning when you are ready for breakfast, you phone reception to let them know when you would like a tray brought to your room. The decor in the guest rooms varies. Many have been refurbished while others, although the style might seem a bit dated, remain the same as they have for years because the loyal guests protest any proposed changes to their favorite rooms - they love everything *exactly* as it is. *Directions:* Take the Ocean Avenue exit from highway 1, turn right on Dolores street and Vagabond's House Inn is on the corner of 4th Street.

VAGABOND'S HOUSE INN
Innkeeper: Honey Jones
Dolores & 4th Street, P.O. Box 2747
Carmel, CA 93921
Tel: (408) 624-7738
11 bedrooms with private bathrooms
Double from $75 to $125
Open: all year
Credit cards: all major
Children accepted over 12

Threading into the hills east of Carmel is the beautiful Carmel Valley where, unlike Carmel which tends to be foggy, almost every day is blessed with sunshine. Here, tucked into its own 330-acre oasis, is Stonepine, built by the Crockers, an early-California dynasty of great wealth. Anticipation of the very special treat awaiting builds as impressive, wrought-iron gates magically open, allowing you to enter. The road crosses a small bridge then winds through the trees, ending in the courtyard of a beautiful home, Italian in feel with a muted pink facade accented with red tile roof, shuttered windows and fancy grille-work. Inside, a quiet elegance oozes from every niche and corner. No expense is spared in the splendid furnishings which give no hint that this is a commercial operation. You definitely feel like a guest in a private mansion as you roam from library to sitting room to dining room, each decorated to perfection. The dining room, handsomely lined in mellow antique panelling, is set exquisitely for dinner each night with fine crystal and china. Upstairs are eight beautiful bedrooms - four more are in the guest house. Although there is a swimming pool and a tennis court, Stonepine was built as a ranch, and horses are the main attraction. As you might have guessed, the Stonepine is very expensive. It is worth every penny. *Directions:* Watch for the sign to the right after leaving Carmel Valley Village going east on G 16.

STONEPINE
Innkeeper: Dirk Oldenburg
150 E. Carmel Valley Road
Carmel Valley, CA 93924
Tel: (408) 659-2245
2 bedrooms & 10 suites with private bathrooms
Double from $150 to $500
Open: all year
Credit cards: all major
Children accepted

The Garden House Inn, a most appealing white, three-story house, brightly trimmed with green, is conveniently situated just a two-minute walk to Avalon's waterfront. As soon as you enter, you immediately realize that the attractiveness is more than skin deep - all the rooms are bright and pretty and show the loving attention to detail of the owners, the Olsen family, who are no strangers to Catalina - they have owned a second home here since the 1930s. The idea to open a small hotel was son Jon's, but the success of the operation is definitely a family affair. Jon's parents (Carolyn and Ted) and his sister (Cathy) are all totally involved in making the Garden House Inn very special. But don't get the idea that this is a homespun operation: it is definitely a sophisticated, professionally run establishment. It is the kind of inn conducive to making friends with other guests. When the weather is nippy, guests congregate about a corner fireplace in the lounge, but, when the sun is out, the favorite spot is the garden terrace set with tables and umbrellas. Upstairs the bedrooms vary in size and decor: all are sunny and pretty and show the clever hand of a professional decorator. In the evening wine and hors d'oeuvres are complimentary and in the morning a delicious cold buffet is served. *Directions:* Boat or plane to Avalon and then taxi to the hotel. Boats to Catalina leave from Balboa, Long Beach, San Pedro and San Diego.

GARDEN HOUSE INN
Innkeepers: Cathy & Carolyn Olsen
125 Claressa
Avalon, Catalina Island, CA 90704
Tel: (213) 510-0356
7 bedrooms with private bathrooms
Double from $125 to $225
Open: all year
Credit cards: MC, VS
Children accepted over 16

Staying at The Inn on Mt Ada is like stepping into a fairytale - suddenly you are "King of the Mountain". This is not too far from reality, since the inn is the beautiful Wrigley family mansion (chewing gum, you know), their vacation "cottage" built high on the hill overlooking Avalon harbor. If you arrive by ferry at Catalina Island (the most romantic approach), you cannot miss the house: as your boat pulls into the bay, the mansion appears like a white wedding cake to your left above the harbor. The inn is expensive, but one shouldn't think about money because, once through the door, you have bought a dream. You are truly like a pampered guest in a millionaire's home, with hardly a hint of commercialism (until you pay the bill) to put a damper to the illusion. The lounges and dining room have been redecorated with soft, pretty colors and traditional furniture and fabrics appropriate to the era when the house was built. Upstairs are six individually decorated bedrooms, the grandest having a fireplace, sitting area and a terrace with breathtaking views of the harbor. Rates include all the extras such as complimentary use of your own little golf cart or free taxi service, scrumptious breakfast, afternoon tea and, in the evening, hors d'oeuvres and wine. *Directions:* Boat or plane to Avalon and then taxi to the hotel. Boats to Catalina leave from Balboa, Long Beach, San Pedro and San Diego.

INN ON MT ADA
Innkeepers: Marlene McAdam & Suzie Griffin
1 Wrigley Road
Avalon, Catalina, CA 90704
Tel: (213) 510-2030
6 bedrooms with private bathrooms
Double from $220 to $440
Open: all year
Credit cards: all major
Children accepted over 14

Ye Olde Shelford House, a stately, white Victorian farmhouse dating back to the 1880s, is located just to the east of Cloverdale, perched on a small knoll overlooking fields of grapes. A large porch, complete with an old-fashioned swing, wraps around the front of the home. Downstairs the parlor is very formal, decorated with fussy Victorian furniture. Upstairs there are two fresh and pretty bedrooms which share a large bathroom. A downstairs bedroom has a private bathroom. On all of the beds there are beautiful quilts - every one of them lovingly sewn by Ina Sauder. Behind the main home is a newly constructed annex where three more guest rooms are built above the carriage house. These rooms each have a private bathroom and share a parlor. The bedroom in front has a real country view out over the pool to the horse corral and fields of grapes. In the corral you will probably spot Brandy and Casey, the horses who pull an old-fashioned, turn-of-the-century surrey. Upon prior arrangement (and of course at extra charge), Al will hitch up the surrey and take guests on tours to some of the surrounding vineyards. When you return from wine touring, the pool is most inviting on a hot day. *Directions:* Take the main street through the town of Cloverdale, highway 101, and turn east on First Street to River Road. After going over the bridge, you see the inn on your right.

YE OLDE SHELFORD HOUSE
Innkeepers: Ina and Al Sauder
29955 River Road
Cloverdale, CA 95425
Tel: (707) 894-5956
6 bedrooms, 4 with private bathrooms
Double from $85 to $95
Open: all year
Credit cards: MC, VS
Children accepted

For travellers driving along California's seemingly endless interstate between San Francisco and Los Angeles, the Harris Ranch offers a welcome break in a long tedious drive, the opportunity for an overnight stay. The ranch has long been famous for the excellent beef it produces from the over 100,000 cattle on the Harris Ranch feed lot and sage travellers for years have calculated their departure to reach Coalinga in time for either lunch or dinner. Recently the Harris family has added accommodations in a building reminiscent of an early California hacienda, tempting travellers to overnight on their way between California's two metropolises. Siena-wash stucco walls, red-tile roofs and arched windows decorate the exterior while light scrubbed-pine furniture and fresh country floral prints adorn lovely and very commodious guest rooms. Bordering a 25 meter pool on three sides, almost all bedrooms overlook the central patio, garden and pool. On Saturday afternoons, the practice of serving margaritas poolside has already become a tradition. The greatest surprise at the inn is the price: for almost the same cost of a noisy freeway motel, you can enjoy the elegance and quiet of the ranch. *Directions:* Harris Ranch is midway between San Francisco and Los Angeles where I-5 crosses highway 198.

INN AT HARRIS RANCH
Innkeepers: John & Carole Harris
Route 1, P.O. Box 777
Coalinga, CA 93210
Tel: (209) 935-0717
89 bedrooms with private bathrooms
Double from $74 to $195
Open: all year
Credit cards: all major
Children accepted

The Coloma Country Inn, a handsome early-American farmhouse, was built in 1852, four years after gold was discovered at Sutter's Mill which is located just down the street. Today Coloma is a sleepy little village where the scant remains of the heady gold rush days are separated by wide green lawns which give it the air of being a well-kept park sloping up from the American River. The Coloma Country Inn sits in the middle of the park, its wrap-around porch inviting guests to relax and sip a glass of wine while soaking in the beauty of the surrounding tranquil countryside. Inside the decor is perfectly lovely, a very simple, very effective American country style, though some rooms do have some Victorian pieces. All the beds are doubles and each is accented by a lovely antique quilt from Cindi's large collection. Behind the inn is an attractive small pond with a little boat moored at the dock. The surrounding gold country is a great attraction to visitors to these parts, but, if you are looking for alternate means of transportation, Alan, a commercial, hot air balloon pilot, can arrange to take you aloft. If you are game for further excitement he can arrange one- or two-day raft trips on the nearby river. *Directions:* Take highway 50 from Sacramento to Placerville, then exit on highway 49 heading north for the 8-mile drive to Coloma.

COLOMA COUNTRY INN
Innkeepers: Cindi & Alan Ehrgott
High St, P.O. Box 502
Coloma, CA 95613
Tel: (916) 622-6919
5 bedrooms, 3 with private bathrooms
Doubles from $68 to $75
Open: all year
Credit cards: none accepted
Children accepted

Columbia is a state-preserved gold-rush town whose shops and stores have been re-created to show life in the heyday of the California gold rush. On Main Street is the exquisitely restored City Hotel. Prior to 1874 the building was a gold assay office, the state company headquarters, an opera house and a newspaper office. Now it is owned by the State of California and staffed by students from Columbia College's hotel management program (consequently the staff, dressed in their period costumes, are exceedingly young and wonderfully friendly). The excellent restaurant and the conviviality of the adjacent What Cheer Bar provide an especially pleasant way to spend an evening. The high-ceilinged bedrooms have Victorian or early-American furniture. The very nicest rooms open directly onto the parlor, rooms 1 and 2 having the added attraction of balconies overlooking Main Street. All the bedrooms have private en-suite toilets and washbasin. It is not a problem to have showers down the hallway when slippers, robes and little wicker baskets to carry soap, shampoo and towels are provided. A simple Continental breakfast is served on the buffet in the parlor. *Directions:* From the San Francisco area take highway 580 for 60 miles, then 120 east to Sonora and highway 49 north from Sonora for the 4-mile drive to Columbia.

CITY HOTEL
Manager: Tom Bender
Main Street
Columbia State Historic Park, CA 95310
Tel: (209) 532-1479
9 bedrooms with 1/2 baths
Showers down the hall
Double from \$60 to \$75
Open: all year
Credit cards: all major
Children accepted

The Fallon Hotel is owned and operated in the same way as the nearby City Hotel in this gem of a gold-rush town. The hotel opened in 1986 after experiencing a $4,000,000 refurbishment from the State of California. The bedrooms are perfect reflections of the opulent 1880s, with patterned ceilings, colorful, ornate wallpaper and grand antique furniture. Front rooms have shaded balconies. All have en-suite pull-chain toilets and ornate washbasins. Like the nearby City Hotel, showers are down the hall and slippers, bathrobes and baskets of toiletries are handily provided. One downstairs room has wider doors for wheelchair access. A simple buffet-style Continental breakfast is served in the adjoining ice cream parlor. In the Fallon Hotel building is the Fallon Theater, offering a year-round schedule of contemporary dramas, musicals and melodramas. When making reservations at either the City or Fallon Hotels ask about their excellent value-for-money theater and dinner packages. *Directions:* From the San Francisco area take highway 580 for 60 miles, then 120 east to Sonora and highway 49 north from Sonora for the 4-mile drive to Columbia which is off the main highway.

FALLON HOTEL
Manager: Tom Bender
Washington Street
Columbia State Historic Park, CA 95310
Tel: (209) 532-1470
13 bedrooms with 1/2 baths
Showers down the hall
Double from $55 to $75
Open: all year
Credit cards: all major
Children accepted

The Rock Haus Inn was built in 1911 for the Keller family and their ten children - in its heyday it was one of the most impressive homes in this attractive seaside town. Because the home is set on a small hill many of the rooms overlook the ocean several blocks away. The entrance is off the verandah, a closed-in porch on the ocean side of the house where homemade muffins, warm strudel and fresh fruit are offered for breakfast. Just inside, the living room, decorated in light, airy colors has chairs set before a large brick fireplace: afternoon refreshments are served here. Each of the ten bedrooms is completely different in theme and decor, but all beds are decked with wonderful goosedown comforters and have the extras of bottled water, fresh flowers, apples and candy. Triple Crown is a large room, in tans and blues, it has a king bed, large armchairs, a large dressing area and white shuttered windows that look out to the ocean. A favorite room on the second floor is the Whale Watch whose bed, angled to maximize the view, has a blue and white striped duvet cover. A wooden whale hangs in the room to set the theme. Another lovely room, the Huntsman, has its own brick fireplace, a king bed and a red plaid flannel duvet. *Directions*: From Los Angeles drive south on highway 5, exit Via Dela Valle and head west turning left at the first signal onto Jimmy Duarante Boulevard which you follow to 15th Street where you turn left.

ROCK HAUS INN
Innkeeper: Doris Holmes
410 Fifteenth Street
Del Mar, CA 92014
Tel: (619) 481-3764
10 bedrooms, 4 with private bathrooms
Double from $75 to $135
Open: all year
Credit cards: all major
Inappropriate for children

Seemingly tucked miles away in the countryside, Brookside Farm is actually only a 35-five minute drive from the outskirts of San Diego. Edd and Judy Guishard have done a remarkable job of converting an ordinary complex of farm buildings into an inviting inn. Judy is an artist and has painted most of the inn's pictures. She also made the quilts and decorated each room, letting its location and mood set its theme: the Bird's Nest tucked under the eaves has lovely bird stenciling on the walls, while Captain Small's room has a red and blue quilt and blue checked chairs. The original well house is now the Hunter's Cabin and has a rustic decor, woodburning stove, planked floors and overlooks the creek through a wall of paned windows and screened porch. Edd is just as creative and is responsible for the inn's stained glass windows as well as being a wonderful chef. On weekends he prepares an inviting four-course dinner, inviting guests to share in the preparation (he owned several restaurants in the San Diego area before moving here). The setting of the inn is lovely: you can play badminton on the lawn, laze away the hours on the patio or relax in the spa under the grape arbor. *Directions:* From San Diego take highway 94 east to Dulzura, go 1 1/2 miles past the cafe and turn right on Marron Valley Road.

BROOKSIDE FARM B & B INN
Innkeepers: Edd & Judy Guishard
1373 Marron Valley Road
Dulzura, CA 92017
Tel: (619) 468-3043
9 bedrooms, 4 with private bathrooms
Double from $45 to $65
Open: all year
Credit cards: none accepted
Inappropriate for children

The Elk Cove Inn dates back to 1883 when it was built by the L. E. White Lumber Company in a meadow overlooking the sea. While many lumber companies built large, impressive mansions, L. E. White built a small, whimsical, white Victorian with a steep mansard roof. The setting is superb, high on a bluff overlooking a very wide expanse of driftwood-strewn beach, happily accessible by a path winding down the hill. The owner, German born Hildrun Triebess, lives in the main house which is the private residence of her family. However, her home is open to guests each morning when breakfast is served in the dining room whose windows overlook the sea. Behind the house two little white guest cottages perch on the edge of the bluff. Adjacent to these is a new, two-unit, natural wood cottage. All the rooms are cozy and have woodburning fireplaces or stoves and lovely views. Everywhere one notices special "Hildrun touches" such as fresh flowers, hand-embroidered linens and sun-dried sheets and towels. This is a simple inn: nothing fancy, but most inviting. *Directions:* Drive north from San Francisco on highway 101 to Cloverdale, turn west on highway 128 to highway 1, then south 5 miles to the Elk Cove Inn.

ELK COVE INN
Innkeeper: Hildrun-Uta Triebess
6300 South Highway One
Elk, CA 95432
Tel: (707) 877-3321
6 bedrooms with private bathrooms
Double from $88 to $168
Open: all year
Credit cards: none accepted
Children accepted over 12

The Harbor House has a fantastic location - on one of the prettiest bluffs along the Mendocino coast. There is even a little path, with benches along the way, winding down the cliff to a secluded private beach. The home was built in 1916 as a guest house for the Goodyear Redwood Lumber Company, so it is no wonder to find everything inside and outside built of redwood. The inn is extremely appealing, reflecting the ambiance of a beautiful, elegant country lodge. You enter into a charming redwood-panelled living room dominated by a large fireplace which is also made of redwood. An Oriental carpet, comfortable sofas, beamed ceiling, soft lighting and a piano tucked in the corner add to the inviting warmth. Doors lead from the lounge to the verandah-like dining room, stretching the length of the building, with big picture windows looking out to the sea. A broad wooden staircase leads upstairs to comfortably furnished, homey bedrooms, some with fireplaces and magnificent views. Other guest rooms are located in the adjacent cottages. Included in the room rate are both dinner and breakfast - and the food is terrific: home-baked breads, freshly ground coffee, garden vegetables and, of course, wonderful fish. *Directions:* Take highway 101 north from San Francisco to Cloverdale, 128 west to the ocean and highway 1 south for 5 miles to Elk.

HARBOR HOUSE - INN BY THE SEA
Innkeepers: Helen & Dean Turner
5600 South Highway One
Elk, CA 95432
Tel: (707) 877-3203
10 bedrooms with private bathrooms
Double from $135 to $200 - includes dinner
Open: all year
Credit cards: none accepted
Children accepted over 16

The Carter House Country Inn is not old, but it is certainly appears to be. This is not surprising since it is an exact copy of an early Victorian home built in San Francisco. The inn is the dream of Mark Carter who grew up in Eureka admiring her many Victorian beauties. He decided to build an inn using the original plans he had found for a Victorian house designed by the same architect who built the Carson Mansion (a huge, sensational Victorian showplace in Eureka). Mark and his wife, Christi, personally manage the entire operation. Christi, an excellent chef, has gained national recognition for the outstanding dinners as well as breakfasts. The decor is in keeping with the exterior. The small Victorian parlor, where guests are served wine and hors d'oeuvres at 6:00PM and nightcaps at bedtime, looks as if it were straight out of the 19th century. The bedrooms are comfortable, each with an antique ambiance. Best yet, there are down comforters, fluffy pillows and cozy flannel robes to make guests really feel "at home". Mark and Christi also own the Hotel Carter located catty-corner across the street where you will find a gourmet restaurant (Christi has a hand in the kitchen) and also very attractive guest rooms decorated with antique and reproduction light pine furniture. *Directions:* Take highway 101 north to Eureka. The highway turns into Fifth Street. From Fifth Street, turn left on L Street and go 2 blocks.

THE CARTER HOUSE
Innkeepers: Mark & Christi Carter
1033 Third Street
Eureka, CA 95501
Tel: (707) 445-1390
7 bedrooms, 3 with private bathrooms
Double from $65 to $120
Open: all year
Credit cards: all major
Children accepted over 12

Ferndale is a jewel - a wonderfully preserved Victorian town 5 miles from the northern California coast. Happily, for those who want to immerse themselves in the nostalgia of days-gone-by, accommodations are available in The Gingerbread Mansion, an inn oozing with Victorian ambiance. Within this restored fantasy of turrets and gables lies a small hotel of great sophistication: the bath water is instantly hot, the towels lush, the beds comfortable, reading lamps properly placed, beds turned down each night, chocolates on the pillow, bathrobes tucked in the wardrobe. Many of the bedrooms are very elaborate; several have extra fancy bathrooms. Our favorites, however, were the less extravagantly furnished guest rooms, which also happen to be less expensive. Like the house, the beautiful garden is meticulously groomed. The flower beds abound with color and the formal hedges are trimmed to perfection. However, all is not stiffly formal: bits of whimsy such as "his and hers" clawfoot tubs in two of the bedrooms and bicyles painted to match the inn insert a bit of lightheartedness. For guests desiring a longer stay, Ken and Wendy also offer a two-bedroom cottage with kitchen just two blocks from town in its own little meadow. *Directions:* Take highway 101 north to the Fernbridge/Ferndale exit. Go 5 miles to Main Street, turn left at the Bank of America and go one block.

THE GINGERBREAD MANSION
Innkeepers: Wendy Hatfield & Ken Torbert
400 Berding Street
Ferndale, CA 95536
Tel: (707) 786-4000
9 bedrooms with private bathrooms
Double from $75 to $150
Open: all year
Credit cards: MC, VS
Children accepted over 10

You would think you are in England instead of northern California when you first see the large, Tudor-style Benbow Inn. The English theme continues as you step inside the lounge with its large antique fireplace flanked by comfortable sofas, antique chests, paintings, needlepoint, cherrywood wainscoting, two grandfather clocks, potted green plants and a splendid Oriental carpet. At tea time complimentary English tea and scones are served along with mulled wine when the days are nippy. The dining room too is very English: a beautiful, sunny room with beamed ceiling and dark oak Windsor chairs. Both the reception hall and the dining room open out to a pretty courtyard overlooking the river. The traditionally decorated bedrooms vary in size - all the way from small rooms to spacious suites with fireplaces, wet bars and private jacuzzis. There are bedrooms located both in the main hotel and in an annex which also opens onto the courtyard. The one disadvantage of the Benbow Inn is its proximity to the freeway, but loyal guests do not seem to mind. A wonderful feature here is the very special Christmas celebration - events including Christmas movies, carolling and dancing are planned each day, and there is a very festive English Christmas dinner. *Directions:* Drive north on 101. Just south of Garberville, take the Benbow exit. You will see the hotel to the west of the freeway.

BENBOW INN
Innkeeper: Patsy Watts
445 Lake Benbow Drive
Garberville, CA 95440
Tel: (707) 923-2124
55 bedrooms with private bathrooms
Double from $78 to $220
Closed: January 2 to mid-April
Credit cards: all major
Children accepted

Georgetown's unusually wide, tree-lined streets faced by wood-frame buildings give character and charm to this backwater town perched high on a hill above the South Fork of the American River. The American River Inn was once a boarding house for gold miners who came to make their fortune, but they certainly did not have today's luxuries of a spa and swimming pool. The main house is a picture-perfect Victorian whose interior beautifully complements the lovely exterior. Inside the spacious, individually decorated bedrooms are furnished with antiques appropriate to the period and the bathrooms have clawfoot tubs and pull-chain toilets. A nifty-gifty shop occupies a small front room. A full breakfast is served in the dining room or on the patio and guests have the use of a comfortable lounge. Across the lawn and past the swimming pool and spa is the Queen Ann House which is perfect for groups or wedding parties. A more recent addition to the complex are the Woodside Mine Suites in a very 20th-century building where the addition of country-cute decor cannot overcome aluminum windows and modern architecture. The inn is happy to make arrangements for whitewater rafting, kayaking, bicycling or hot air ballooning. *Directions:* From Sacramento take highway 50 to Placerville, then the 49 north to the 193 which brings you into Georgetown. The American River Inn is on Main Street.

AMERICAN RIVER INN
Innkeepers: Neal & Carol Lamonte
P.O. Box 43, Main at Orleans Street
Georgetown, CA 95634
Tel: (916) 333-4499
25 bedrooms, 12 with private bathrooms
Double from $66 to $78
Open: all year
Credit cards: all major
Children accepted over 8

It is hard not to notice Beltane Ranch, a pale yellow clapboard house encircled on both stories by broad verandahs, set on the hillside off the Valley of the Moon Road. Rosemary, the owner, will probably be in the cozy country kitchen when you arrive, but if she is away from home she will write you a welcoming note on the chalkboard hung by the back door. The house has no internal staircase, so each room has a private entrance off the verandah - which was probably a very handy thing when this was the weekend retreat of a San Francisco madam. Incidentally, this also explains the rather southern architecture of the house as "madam" hailed from Louisiana. The bedrooms have a very comfortable, family feel to them: handsome beds, lovely old quilts, homey tables and chairs. Chairs are placed on the verandah outside each room and offer a wonderful spot to settle and enjoy peaceful countryside views beyond Rosemary's well-tended garden. The home has been in Rosemary's family for many years and she has fond memories of racing round and round the balconies with her siblings - she has always loved this home,so she jumped at the opportunity to turn it into a bed and breakfast. *Directions:* From Sonoma take highway 12 towards Santa Rosa: Beltane Ranch is on your right shortly after passing the turnoff to Glen Ellen.

BELTANE RANCH
Innkeeper: Rosemary Wood
11775 Sonoma Highway
Glen Ellen, CA 95442
Tel: (707) 996-6501
4 bedrooms with private bathrooms
Double from $75 to $90
Closed: January
Credit cards: none accepted
Children accepted over 5

Grass Valley has continued to prosper since the heady gold rush days when Cornish miners arrived from England seeking their fortunes in gold. Although the town cannot compete for charm with adjacent Nevada City, it certainly has a first-class hostelry in Murphy's Inn - this small inn, its broad verandah decorated with topiary ivy baskets, was once the mansion of North Star Mine owner Edward Colman. It has been lovingly restored and refurbished by Marc and Rose Murphy who have subsequently added the houses on two other corners of the street to the inn: one is their home and the other has two large suites which can accommodate guests travelling with children. Bedrooms in the main house range from Theodosia's Suite with its king-size brass bed draped in lace sitting before the fireplace to a small upstairs bedroom that shares a bath. One room just off the kitchen has a delightful pot-belly stove and sunny skylights. The entire inn is furnished in Victorian finery. Marc encourages guests to make themselves at home and stocks the refrigerator with juices, sodas and goodies. He also prepares a hearty breakfast while chatting with his guests. The "swim spa" on the back verandah is heated like a spa in the winter and used as a small pool in the summer. *Directions:* From the San Francisco area take the I-80 to the 49 north to Grass Valley, exit on Colfax, then go left on South Auburn and left on Neal.

MURPHY'S INN
Innkeepers: Marc & Rose Murphy
318 Neal Street
Grass Valley, CA 95945
Tel: (916) 273-6873
9 bedrooms, 7 with private bathrooms
Double from $58 to $118
Open: all year
Credit cards: all major
Children accepted in annex suites

Many of the hotels in this guide have been converted from buildings previously used for other purposes. Not so with the Old Milano Hotel: it has been taking guests since the first day the doors opened in 1905. Although built upon a bluff overlooking the ocean in what appears to be quite an isolated location, at the turn of the century the hotel was in the center of activity, serving overnight stagecoach guests, lumber barons and travellers on their way up the coast by train. Today, the old hotel has been beautifully restored reflecting its original Victorian elegance. The large dining room and wine parlor, with a large stone fireplace, are especially attractive. From Wednesday through Sunday gourmet dinners are served (be sure to make reservations in advance). None of the six guest rooms upstairs has a private bath, but all are attractively decorated with Victorian antiques and most have outstanding views of the ocean. On the first floor is a lavish suite (with a memorable view) where the original owners, the Lucchinetti family, lived. A room is tucked into a cottage in the rear garden and another into an old-fashioned train caboose set amongst the trees. Although it has many attributes, the hotel's most outstanding feature is its perfect location on a lawn which sweeps down to a bluff overlooking the ocean. *Directions:* The Old Milano Hotel is on the Coastal Highway just north of Gualala.

OLD MILANO HOTEL
Innkeeper: Leslie Linscheid
38300 Highway One
Gualala, CA 95445
Tel: (707) 884-3256
9 bedrooms, 3 with private bathrooms
Double from $75 to $160
Open: all year
Credit cards: all major
Inappropriate for children

Until converted to a small inn, The Estate was a private residence. The present owners, Jim Caron and Darryl Notter, have converted it into a small, European-style hotel - not trendy, just quietly elegant. Although sophisticated, the atmosphere is one of a country lodge, with a large stone fireplace opening on two sides, warming both the living room and a cheerful glassed-in sun porch. Just off the living room is a dining room with an enormous crystal chandelier hanging above a central table surrounded by individual small tables. In addition to breakfast, the Estate is now offering dinners for their guests. The dinners are optional and feature fresh Sonoma County produce, much of it grown in the hotel's own gardens. Windows look out from the dining room to a wooded area and a lovely swimming pool on the terrace. The bedrooms are all individual in their decor, just as if you were staying in a private home. Their price reflects the size and location, although each one has a TV, direct-dial phone, and comfortable queen-sized bed decked with down comforter and pillows. The furnishings are elegant, slightly formal but still showing the homey touch of the owners. In fact, Darryl designed and his mother (Mary) hand-sewed the covers on the comforters, the draperies and even the slip-covers on the chairs. The inn is absolutely immaculate and well-tended, a result of owners always present and caring. *Directions:* On highway 116, 1/2 mile south of the bridge as you leave Guerneville.

THE ESTATE
Innkeepers: Jim Caron & Darryl Notter
13555 Highway 116, Guerneville, CA 95446
Tel: (707) 869-9093
10 bedrooms with private bathrooms
Double from $100 to $150
Open: all year
Credit cards: all major
Inappropriate for children

On the hillside across from the Simi Winery, the Belle de Jour Inn is set in its own quiet world. A complex of old farm cottages built in 1873, buffered from the busy main road by a long drive shaded by pine trees and bordered by lush lawn, backing onto a hillside planted with vines, this inn offers an inviting countryside retreat. The complex has four cottages of guest rooms and a single-story farmhouse that is Tom and Brenda's home. Once the grain and tack room, the Caretaker's Suite has a pine four-poster, king-size canopy bed topped with battenberg lace and French doors that open onto a trellised deck. The Fireplace Room is charming and has a bench outside positioned to look out over vineyards. The Morning Hill Room is cozy with a wood stove and a shuttered window seat. The Atelier is large and lovely, but it is the only room whose outdoor area does not overlook the vineyards. A full country breakfast is served in the owners' kitchen or on the front porch, or delivered to your room in a fancy picnic basket. For a memorable wine tasting experience, Tom will take you in his 1923 vintage auto along the backroads of the wine country. Return for a gourmet picnic lunch at the inn and perhaps a refreshing afternoon dip in the cleverly cut-down wine cask, complete with rubber ducky. *Directions:* Going north, exit highway 101 at Dry Creek Road and go east to Healdsburg Avenue. Turn left at the lights and go north for about 1 mile.

BELLE DE JOUR INN
Innkeepers: Tom & Brenda Hearn
16276 Healdsburg Avenue
Healdsburg, CA 95448
Tel: (707) 433-7892
4 bedrooms with private bathrooms
Double from $85 to $125
Open: all year
Credit cards: MC, VS
Inappropriate for children

Haydon House is set in a very quiet neighborhood of Healdsburg four blocks from the main plaza of this especially nice town. Like the town, the Haydon House is most attractive: a lovely, soft-blue Victorian with a crisp, white trim, fronted by a white picket fence heavily laden with pink roses. The main house has a lovely country living room, sitting room and dining area for guests' use. The six bedrooms are like a breath of fresh air - beautifully decorated with homey, comfortable furnishings. At the rear of the lovely garden, to the right of the main house, is a Victorian-style cottage with two large guest rooms occupying the upper floor. As an added touch of luxury the bathrooms in the cottage have double whirlpool bathtubs. A sample of a morning's outstanding breakfast buffet includes fresh orange juice, fresh fruits in season with a special topping of cream yoghurt, muffins, green chili and sausage strata, mushroom and artichoke heart frittata, apple, raisin, nut muffins with orange butter, cinnamon pecan rolls, coffee or tea - a bounty and enough nourishment to last you through a day of wine tasting. *Directions:* When travelling north on highway 101 take the Central Healdsburg exit. Travel straight ahead to the light at Matheson, turn right and continue to Fitch, then turn right on Fitch to Haydon, then left on Haydon.

HAYDON HOUSE
Innkeepers: Joanne & Richard Claus
321 Haydon Street
Healdsburg, CA 95448
Tel: (707) 433-5228
8 bedrooms, 4 with private bathrooms
Double from $70 to $110
Open: all year
Credit cards: MC, VS
Children accepted over 10

Healdsburg's main square is a green park bordered by shops and restaurants. If you want to stay in this charming town you can do no better than the Healdsburg Inn on the Plaza. The entrance is through an awning-covered door into a freshly painted, high-ceilinged reception that doubles as an art gallery - watercolor floral prints were on display when we visited. A dramatic, long flight of stairs winds up to a central salon where a jigsaw puzzle is left for each successive guest to work a bit on. Off the salon are nine bedrooms decorated in a very Victorian decor, a few of which overlook the old plaza through bay windows. An enclosed rooftop room has white tables and chairs, lots of greenery and colorful Oriental carpets. There are two breakfast servings: at 8:00AM cereal, toast, jam and beverages are available for early risers and at 9:00AM a hot egg dish is served. Plan on arriving around 4:00PM to enjoy cakes, cookies, pies and lemonade: complimentary wine and fresh buttered popcorn are served at 6:00PM. Saturday night rates are $10 higher and include a spectacular Sunday brunch. The Inn on the Plaza is a very friendly, welcoming hotel and Genny or her daughter Dyanne are usually there to greet you. *Directions:* The inn is on the south side of Healdsburg's main plaza.

HEALDSBURG INN ON THE PLAZA
Innkeeper: Genny Jenkins
116 Matheson
Healdsburg, CA 95448
Tel: (707) 433-6991
10 bedrooms, 9 with private bathrooms
Double from $65 to $120
Open: all year
Credit cards: all major
Children accepted over 10

The Madrona Manor is a very special small hotel. It really has everything: the location is superb - crowning a small hill in the country, yet just minutes from Healdsburg; the building is spectacular - a fantasy gingerbread mansion; the grounds are glorious - 8 acres of manicured gardens; the rooms in the manor are beautiful - filled with authentic Victorian antiques; the warm days are anticipated - a lovely pool nestles in the garden; the food is gourmet - Todd Muir is a fabulous chef who has been featured in *Gourmet*. But the greatest asset of the hotel are the owners, Carol and John Muir. They bought the property in 1981 and spent two years of love and labor converting it into a commercially successful, sophisticated little hotel without losing any of the warmth and graciousness of a tiny homespun inn. Carol and John really care and it shows in every detail from the well-trained staff to the immaculate guest rooms where, although the beds might be antique, the mattresses are firm and the linens of the finest quality. The entire family is involved in the operation. Son Todd is the renowned chef, son Mark worked on the renovations, son-in-law John Fitzgerald was the landscape architect, son Rob is a partner in the business. *Directions:* Driving north on highway 101, take the Central Healdsburg exit, turn left at the intersection and go under the freeway. You will be on Westside Road.

MADRONA MANOR
Innkeepers: Carol & John Muir
1001 Westside Road
Healdsburg, CA 95448
Tel: (707) 433-4231
20 bedrooms with private bathrooms
Double from $87.50 to $130
Open: all year
Credit cards: all major
Children accepted

Idyllwild is a mile-high village of some three thousand residents, and with its magnificent hiking trails affords a wonderful weekend getaway from the city. The Fern Valley Inn is a rustic lodge of log cabins set under clear blue skies and surrounded by pine trees. Dan and Sherrell LaMont personally manage the inn and care for their guests. Sherrell is responsible for the individual decor in the cottages, each of which is furnished with antiques, handmade quilts or spreads and equipped with a refrigerator, hidden-away television and a working fireplace or log stove. Themes vary from a western motif to The School Room with its old school prints, a drawing slate and printed rules for teachers. Rooms are supplied with coffee, tea, fruit and a basket of nutbreads as breakfast fare. The grounds are immaculately kept - swept pathways wind amongst the cottages, leading to the central pool, rose garden and parlor. The parlor with its porch is a welcoming place for guests to congregate - a decanter of sherry, backgammon, Scrabble and puzzles are always left out. A fire burns every evening during winter months. At Thanksgiving and Christmas, the LaMonts invite their guests to join them for a festive dinner and at Christmas to sing carols round the piano. *Directions:* Take highway 10 west from Los Angeles to Banning and highway 243 to Idyllwild. Turn right on North Circle, right on South Circle, then left on Fern Valley Road.

FERN VALLEY INN
Innkeepers: Dan & Sherrell LaMont
25240 Fern Valley Road, P.O. Box 116
Idyllwild, CA 92349
Tel: (714) 659-2205
12 bedrooms with private bathrooms
Double from $55 to $75
Open: all year
Credit cards: MC, VS
Inappropriate for children

The Strawberry Creek Inn, a lovely dark-shingled building with etched glass windows, sits back off the main road on the final approach to town. It is owner managed, with Jim Goff and Diana Dugan the lovely hosts: Jim's domain is the expansive gardens, while Diana's personal warmth is reflected in the decor - she is responsible for every nook and inviting touch. In the shingled main house the parlor is set with a large comfy sofa, tables and chairs before the fireplace and its bookshelves are brimming with novels and games. Diana has selected coordinating wallpapers, borders and trims in colors of warm beige and greens. Off the parlor in a cheerful, enclosed sun porch, long trestle tables accommodate guests with a bountiful feast - German, French toast with bratwurst, fruit, juice, coffee or tea is just one sample breakfast. The bedrooms are located both in the main house and in a newer back wing that wraps around a sunny courtyard. Each room is decked with country handmade quilts or crocheted spreads. Rooms in the main house, four upstairs and one down, are charming, and those sharing a bath are furnished with plush robes. The courtyard rooms were built with private fireplaces, baths and skylights and equipped with a small refrigerator and queen beds. *Directions:* On the approach to town from the south on highway 243 the Strawberry Creek Inn is located on the right just past South Circle Drive.

STRAWBERRY CREEK INN
Innkeepers: Diana Dugan & Jim Goff
26370 Highway 243, P.O. Box 1818
Idyllwild, CA 92349
Tel: (714) 659-3202
9 bedrooms, all with private bathrooms
Double from $70 to $90
Open: all year
Credit cards: MC, VS
Inappropriate for children

The Blackthorne Inn is the whimsical creation of Susan and Bill Wigert. They have built a Hansel and Gretel house tucked among the tree tops, loaded with peaked roofs, dormer windows, funny little turrets, bay windows and an octagonal tower. You wind up through the trees to the main entry level which is wrapped by an enormous wooden deck, emphasizing the treehouse look. The living room is very spacious, dominated by a floor-to-ceiling stone fireplace. Skylights, a stained glass window, a Chinese carpet, wood-panelled walls, baskets of flowers and walls of windows looking out into the trees make the room most appealing. The guest rooms, located on various levels, are attractively decorated, not in any particular period or style, but with a pretty, fresh, country look. The favorite choice of many guests is the Eagle's Nest, located in the octagonal tower, where walls of glass give the impression one is sleeping under the stars - camping at its best. Each of the other guest rooms has its own personality. The Overlook has stained glass windows, The Lupine Room has a private entrance, The Studio has a separate sitting room and The Hideaway (one of our favorites) has a bay window looking out into the trees. *Directions:* From highway 101 take Sir Francis Drake Boulevard to Olema. Turn right for about 2 miles, then left toward Inverness. Go a little over 1 mile and turn left on Vallejo Avenue (at the Knave of Hearts Bakery).

BLACKTHORNE INN
Innkeeper: Susan Wigert
266 Vallejo Avenue
Inverness, CA 94937
Tel: (415) 663-8621
5 bedrooms, 2 with private bathrooms
Double from $105 to $165
Open: all year
Credit cards: MC, VS
Children accepted over 14

Dancing Coyote Beach is a secluded little hideaway just steps from the heart of Inverness. Tucked in a wooded little park, next to their own small sand beach, are three attached, weathered guest houses. Each has its own private entry, a cozy lounge warmed by a wood-burning fireplace and a kitchenette. The most expensive accommodation is the one closest to the bay which has an especially large deck and enjoys unobstructed views over the water. The decor is fresh and pretty - there is no set style, just attractive, color-coordinated fabrics and comfortable furnishings. Chairs and a sofa are grouped around the fireplace in the living room (the sofa converts to a bed). A flight of stairs leads to an upper-level loft bedroom with lovely views through the trees either to the beach or the bay. Breakfast is not included, but each unit has its own kitchen with coffeemaker and coffee provided. The Grey Whale, just a few minutes' walk away, makes scrumptious bakery goods each morning. Dancing Coyote Beach makes a perfect base for exploring the Point Reyes Park: it is located right on the road leading to the lighthouse and yet you have the convenience of being within walking distance of Inverness' restaurants. You also have the wonderful bonus of being right on Tomales Bay. *Directions:* Drive through Inverness and just as you start to leave town, turn down a little driveway to your right, just after you pass the Inverness Cafe on your left.

DANCING COYOTE BEACH
Innkeeper: Kay Ramsey
12794 Sir Francis Drake Blvd
Inverness, CA 94937
Tel: (415) 669-7200
3 cottages
Double from $95 to $125 (without breakfast)
Open: all year
Credit cards: none accepted
Children accepted

Ten Inverness Way is a most attractive-looking inn - a cozy, redwood-shingled building fronted by a carefree, happy English garden. Originally built in 1904 as a family home, it was bought in 1980 by Mary Davies who converted it into an inn - Mary is the very proficient manager. A flagstone path leads from the road up a slope, through the flowerbeds to the front door. Inside, a staircase takes you to the second level and opens to the living room which has an informal ambiance with a large stone fireplace, redwood walls, Oriental carpets, comfortable furnishings and a few antique accents. The room is not elegant nor decorator perfect, but is very inviting. This is where Mary says guests relax and make themselves at home - playing games or snuggling up on the sofa with a good book. As the tensions of city life recede, guests strike up conversations with fellow visitors. The four small bedrooms are simply decorated but fresh and immaculately clean, with handmade quilts on the beds adding a special touch. In the morning Mary serves a delicious full breakfast in the sunny breakfast room, opening through French doors off the living room. After breakfast, Point Reyes National Seashore is just waiting to be explored. *Directions:* Drive into Inverness on the main road, Sir Francis Drake Boulevard, and watch for the sign pointing to your left to Ten Inverness Way.

TEN INVERNESS WAY
Innkeeper: Mary Davies
10 Inverness Way
Inverness, CA 94937
Tel: (415) 669-1648
4 bedrooms with private bathrooms
Double from $95 to $105
Open: all year
Credit cards: MC, VS
Children accepted who behave as adults

Jamestown, with its high wooden sidewalks and wooden store fronts with broad balconies hanging to the street, wears an air of yesteryear - you expect to see old-time cowboys emerging from the saloon and a stagecoach rumbling down its main street. It seems that every gold rush town had a hotel similar to this one, but today few can boast of a city hotel that has received the careful restoration that the Jamestown Hotel has. The outside looks much as it did in its heyday, a simple brick false-front building whose second-story balcony forms a roof above the sidewalk. The lobby, cocktail lounge (where drinks are available in a cozy fireside setting in the evening and breakfast is served in the morning) and dining room occupy the ground floor. The restaurant abounds with the same old-world ambiance as the rest of the hotel and prides itself on serving excellent food. On summer days meals are served on the patio. The bedrooms are quaintly Victorian, neat as new pins. Some are two smaller rooms made into a sitting room and bedroom combination. All have attractive, spotless bathrooms and are named for famous personalities, being decorated with that person in mind - Black Bart, Joaquin Murietta, Lotta Crabtree, Jenny Lind, Buffalo Bill. *Directions:* From the San Francisco area take highway 580 for 60 miles, then 120 east to Jamestown which is just before Sonora.

JAMESTOWN HOTEL
Innkeepers: Michael & Marcia Walsh
P.O. Box 539, 18159 Main Street
Jamestown, CA 95327
Tel: (209) 984-3902
8 bedrooms with private bathrooms
Double from $59 to $95
Open: all year
Credit cards: all major
Children accepted over 7

Julian was founded by ex-confederate soldiers when gold was discovered here in 1869. Albert Robinson, a freed slave and an excellent baker, was befriended by a confederate colonel who financed a restaurant and bakery, which later became a hotel. Albert's business was surprizingly well received in this predominantly confederate town. The Julian Hotel, the sole survivor of this town's several Victorian hotels, is the oldest continously operating hotel in southern California and has had only four owners in its ninety-odd years of operation. Guests today are offered quaint rooms that appear much as they would have in the gold rush days. The owners, Steve and Gig Ballinger, have taken great pride in their project to authenticate as best as possible a decor in keeping with the history and character of the inn. With a selection of stylized Victorian wallpapers, patterned carpets and antique furnishings, they have masterfully and attractively achieved their goal. There are eighteen bedrooms, each named for an individual associated with the inn, varying in size as well as decor. Fans cool the rooms in the summer months. The Parlor, where a buffet breakfast and evenıng tea are served, as well as a lovely native stone terrace patio set with redwood tables and surrounded by gardens are available for guests' use. *Directions:* From San Diego, travel 35 miles east on interstate 8 east, then 22 miles north on highway 79.

JULIAN HOTEL
Innkeepers: Steve & Gig Ballinger
2032 Main Street, P.O. Box 1856
Julian, CA 92036
Tel: (619) 765-0201
18 bedrooms, 5 with private bathrooms
Double from $72 to $135
Open: all year
Credit cards: all major
Children accepted mid-week

Eiler's Inn, although on a busy highway, has been carefully designed so that none of the guest rooms face the traffic, but front onto a central courtyard where, instead of car noises, the only sound is that of the gurgling fountain. This inner brick-paved patio, filled with colorfully blooming plants amd potted greenery, is the heart of the inn where guests gather in the evening for wine and cheeses and again in the morning for a wonderful buffet breakfast. If the weather is chilly, guests congregate around the blazing fire in the front lounge. Frequently, one of the owners, Henk or Annette Wirtz, is present. They were guests themselves at Eiler's Inn many years ago when on holiday from Germany, then, when the inn came on the market, they bought it and returned to stay. Their warmth and hospitality are what really make the inn special. A feeling of camaraderie is somehow established amongst the guests - a mood of warmth and informal friendliness. The bedrooms each differ in decor: my favorites were room 209 with flowered wallpaper and an antique wooden headboard and room 204 with a wine-colored print wallpaper contrasting nicely against a white headboard and wicker chairs. The rooms are pleasant, but not outstanding in decor. However, all the guests seem happy and love both the hotel and its proximity to the beach - just a two-minute walk down the hill. *Directions:* On the coastal highway 1, just south of the town center.

EILER'S INN
Innkeeper: Jonna Iversen
741 South Coast Highway
Laguna Beach, CA 92651
Tel: (714) 494-3004
12 bedrooms with private bathrooms
Double from $105 to $120
Open: all year
Credit cards: all major
Children accepted

From the street The Bed & Breakfast Inn at La Jolla is a nondescript building with a pale peach stucco wash, but behind its facade is a surprizing oasis of luxury. The inn is located a few blocks from the heart of La Jolla's elegant shopping district as well as its lovely beach and directly across the street from public tennis courts. The owners describe their decor as "elegant cottage style": beautiful furnishings, lovely fabrics, handsome prints and splendid antiques have been carefully selected to suit the mood of each room. From the Bird Rock, the smallest and least expensive room, charmingly decorated in Laura Ashley blue and white pinstripes and dainty flowered prints, to the spacious and elegant Holiday room with its canopied four-poster bed, dramatic fireplace and color scheme of white on white with beige accents, each room is unique and inviting. Fresh fruit, sherry and flowers are placed in each guest room. Ten rooms are located in the historic house and six in the annex. On sunny days pass through the arched doorway and laze in the back yard at tables set on a brick patio bordered by grass and flowers. Breakfast is served either in the dining area, on the patio, the sundeck or in your bedroom. *Directions:* From San Diego take route 5 and exit right on La Jolla Village Drive. Turn left on Torrey Pines Road, proceed 2 1/2 miles to Prospect Place. Turn right, drive 9 blocks, then turn left on Draper Avenue.

THE BED & BREAKFAST INN AT LA JOLLA
Innkeeper: Ardath Albee
7753 Draper Avenue
La Jolla, CA 92037
Tel: (619) 456-2066
16 bedrooms, 15 with private bathrooms
Double from $70 to $185
Open: all year
Credit cards: MC, VS
Children accepted over 12

Although Eagle's Landing is a bed and breakfast, it is run so professionally that guests have the feeling that they are indeed in a miniature hotel. There are four guest rooms with private bath and, although each varies in decor, they all maintain a comfy-homey ambiance and are all meticulously kept - everything "neat as a pin". One of the bedrooms, the Lake View Suite, is enormous, with its own fireplace and a spacious private deck with a view of the lake. However, my favorite room is the cozy Woods Room, tucked amongst the trees with its own little terrace and entrance. The living room has a large fireplace in the corner and a splendid long wooden trestle table, big enough for all the guests to gather and share their day's adventures. Just off the dining room is a cozy nook where guests can enjoy breakfast. Speaking of breakfast, Dorothy prides herself on treating her guests to a special brunch on Sunday mornings, a hearty start for exploring the lake which is located a short walk from the hotel. However, since this is a private lake, public access is available only in the town of Arrowhead (about a five-minute drive away) *Directions:* Turn north from highway 18 following signs for Blue Jay. Before you reach the lake, the road splits. Turn left on North Bay and watch for Cedarwood on your left - Eagle's Landing is on the corner of North Bay and Cedarwood.

EAGLE'S LANDING
Innkeeper: Dorothy Stone
P.O. Box 1510
Blue Jay, CA 92317
Tel: (714) 336-2642
4 bedrooms with private bathroom
Double from $75 to $125
Open: all year
Credit cards: none accepted
Inappropriate for children

The Saddleback Inn is tucked into its own wooded oasis just a short stroll from Lake Arrowhead Village. Although the inn dates back almost 70 years, when it was built in the style of an English tavern by two sisters from the Midwest, there is nothing "dated" about this small inn. Its present owners have completely renovated every nook and cranny, creating a slick, very sophisticated hotel. Luckily they have kept the old-world look with the use of a few antiques plus many reproductions. The reception area is located in the main lodge which exudes a Victorian mood in its cozy bar and dining room. The original staircase leads off the lobby to 10 guest rooms, some quite small but all attractive. Scattered throughout the 3 1/2 acres are small cottages connected by pathways which house the remaining guest rooms. All of the rooms are decorated with Laura Ashley fabrics and wallpapers, and each has a jacuzzi tub in the bathroom - a wonderful respite after a day of hiking or sightseeing. The Saddleback Inn appears more "slick" than "homey", but behind its commercial facade is the warmth and personalization of an excellent manager, Liza Colton, who creates the ambiance of a small inn. This hotel is an especially suitable choice when travelling with children, as a pretty beach is within walking distance. *Directions:* From highway 173 take the Lake Arrowhead turnoff. Drive 2 miles. The hotel is on the left at the entrance to Lake Arrowhead Village.

SADDLEBACK INN
Innkeeper: Liza Colton
Lake Arrowhead, CA 92352
Tel: (714) 336-3571
35 bedrooms with private bathrooms
Double from $100 to $145
Open: all year
Credit cards: all major
Children accepted

Glendeven is a charming New England-style farmhouse, built in 1867 by Isaiah Stevens for his bride Rebecca. Today, this beautiful clapboard home, elegant in its simplicity, is owned by Jan (a native of Holland) and his wife Janet who purchased the property in 1977 and created one of the most delightful inns on the Mendocino Coast. From the beginning Jan and Janet have poured their love and work into Glendeven, adding improvements over the years. Not only are they a hardworking couple, but both are very talented designers whose eye for proportion, style and color are apparent in every detail. The main home is the two-story farmhouse, painted a creamy tan and trimmed with crisp white. There are more rooms in the Stevenscroft and, most recently, the 1800s haybarn has been converted into an elegant two-bedroom suite. All of the guest rooms are beautifully decorated and each one is special. Some feature antique beds, others claim a private balcony or fireplace. The gardens too are lovely - the 2-acre property, across the highway from the ocean, has been tranformed into a beautifully tended garden. Whether it be the parklike grounds or the rooms, everything is immaculate and shows the professionalism and caring of Jan and Janet and their gracious staff. *Directions:* On highway 1, on the east side of the highway, just south of Mendocino.

GLENDEVEN
Innkeepers: Jan & Janet deVries
8221 North Highway One
Little River, CA 95456
Tel: (707) 937-0083
11 bedrooms, 10 with private bathrooms
Double from $70 to $140
Open: all year
Credit cards: MC, VS
Children accepted over 8

For over 20 years we have been going to stay at one of our favorite hideaways, the Heritage House, which was built in 1877 by John Dennen, the great-grandfather of Gay Dennen Moore, the present owner. Today it is as wonderful as ever. The same quaint yellow farmhouse, with bright red door and lacework of green ivy, remains the heart of the inn. In 1949, when revisiting the Mendocino Coast, Gay's parents spotted the abandoned family farm, bought it on impulse, and opened their "Heritage House". From the beginning, without any advertising, word has spread about the romance of this secluded hideaway, and now the inn is filled months in advance. Over the years, the number of rooms has expanded. In addition to the few tucked into the old farmhouse, others are clustered about the 37 acres in various small cottages and houses with such colorful names as The Bonnet Shop, Country Store, and The Ice Cream Parlor. Wherever you are, the ocean is nearby because the property slopes gently down to a bluff which drops off into the sea. The walks along the cliffs are fabulous, with the huge waves crashing against the rocky coastline. The Heritage House is one of the few inns in this guide where dinner and breakfast are both included in the room rate. *Directions:* As you drive north toward Mendocino along the Coastal Highway 1, you see the Heritage House well signposted to the left of the road just before you come to Little River.

HERITAGE HOUSE
Innkeeper: Gay Dennen Moore
Little River, CA 95456
Tel: (707) 937-5885
70 bedrooms with private bathrooms
Double from $115 to $280 - includes dinner
Closed: December & January
Credit cards: none accepted
Children accepted

The Salisbury House is conveniently located just off the Santa Monica Freeway (highway 10), making easy access to Los Angeles' freeway network. Although the neighborhood, called Arlington Heights, is not particularly pretty, it is better than most in the area, and the street where the Salisbury House is located is one of the best of the lot. Here many of the homes have a good deal of architectural charm, and among these, Salisbury House is one of the nicest. The house, built in 1909, is square, with an interesting gabled roofline and several bay windows. Stained and leaded glass windows add to the old-world ambiance. Inside, the decor is very pleasant: beamed ceilings, wood panelling and lots of windows set a nice background for attractive, country-style furnishings. In the separate dining room one large table is set where guests enjoy a full hot breakfast. There are five bedrooms: because they were occupied I was not able to see them all, but those I did were prettily decorated. I especially liked the Green Room, newly redone with rose-patterned wallpaper and a four-poster bed. It shares a bathroom but seems a good buy at $60 per night. On the top floor, cozily tucked under the eaves, is the Attic Suite, a spacious suite with a king-sized brass bed and an antique clawfoot tub. *Directions:* Take the Santa Monica Freeway east. Turn off at Western Avenue. Go north over the freeway and turn left on 20th (it is the first street.)

SALISBURY HOUSE
Innkeepers: Si & Alice Torvend
2273 West 20th Street
Los Angeles, CA 90018
Tel: (213) 737-7817
5 bedrooms, 3 with private bathrooms
Double from $60 to $75
Open: all year except December 24, 25
Credit cards: all major
Children accepted over 10

The Terrace Manor occupies a niche of respectability in a downtown multi-ethnic neighborhood where a small crescent street is lined by a few handsome, turn-of-the-century homes - each designated as a historical landmark. The nicest of them all is Terrace Manor, a stately, large home perched formally on a terraced lawn overlooking a tiny park. The home was a showplace in its heyday and remains so today, with beautiful stained-glass windows, dark panelled walls and rich hardwood floors. The decor within perfectly suits the period, with rather ornate, somber Victorian antiques in the sitting room and small TV parlor. Upstairs are five spotlessly clean, nicely decorated bedrooms. The choice one is the very spacious Lydia's Room with an ornate king-sized brass and iron bed and a large bath and dressing room combination. The owners, Shirley and Sandy Spillman, are very gracious and attentive to the needs of their guests. If Sandy looks familiar, don't be surprised: you have probably seen him on many TV commercials. Sandy is also a magician and as his guest you have the opportunity to dine at the exclusive private club, the Magic Castle, where fine magicians perform each night. *Directions:* North on the Harbor Freeway. Take the Santa Monica exit heading west and immediately get in the left lane for the Pico off-ramp. Turn left on Pico to Alvarado Terrace. Off-street parking is provided in an enclosed area.

TERRACE MANOR
Innkeepers: Shirley & Sandy Spillman
1353 Alvarado Terrace
Los Angeles, CA 90006
Tel: (213) 381-1478
5 bedrooms with private bathrooms
Double from $55 to $85
Open: all year
Credit cards: all major
Children accepted over 10

The McCloud Guest House has a wonderful setting - in its own pretty little park, surrounded by green lawn and trees, while in the distance is Mount Shasta, northern California's 14,162-foot giant. The inn is not pretentious, but most attractive in its simplicity. Built entirely of wood, the square building is wrapped with a spacious verandah whose supporting columns reach up to a steeply pitched roof from which little dormer windows peek out into the trees. Built in 1907, the inn was originally the home of J. H. Queal, the president of the McCloud River Lumber Company. After extensive renovations, it reopened as a restaurant on the ground level with five bedrooms upstairs. As you enter the foyer, the massive stone fireplace and wood-panelled walls set the country lodge feeling. Upstairs the guests have their own private parlor highlighted with an ornate pool table from the Hearst collection. The original master bedroom is decorated with flowered wallpaper in soft shades of mauve and pink set off by white wicker chairs. Each of the other guest rooms has its own color scheme. Most have antique white iron beds, but one has a four-poster bed which looks quite handsome against a dark plaid wallpaper. *Directions:* Drive north on highway 5, then go east on highway 89 toward McCloud. Before you reach the village turn left on Colombero Drive.

McCLOUD GUEST HOUSE
Innkeepers: Bill & Patti Leigh
Dennis & Pat Abreu
606 West Colombero Drive
McCloud, CA 96057
Tel: (916) 964-3160
5 bedrooms with private bathrooms
Double from $70 to $95
Open: all year
Credit cards: MC, VS
Inappropriate for children

The Blue Heron Inn is not the typical Mendocino Victorian, but a simple, New England-style house, painted white with blue trim. A white picket fence encloses the garden to each side, completing the cottage look. On the first floor there is a small restaurant (The Chocolate Moosse) and upstairs are two modestly priced, prettily decorated bedrooms sharing a bath, One of the bedrooms is called the Bay Room, a charming corner room with double bed which has a sweeping view of the ocean on one side and village rooftops on the other. The other bedroom is the Sunset Room, a cozy, double-bedded, dormer room. Although tiny, this room is most appealing, with a French writing table tucked beneath the window, puffy comforter on the bed, a wicker sofa, and a beautiful ocean view. In an attached cottage, reached by its own private entrance, is a third bedroom, the Garden Room, which has a queen-sized bed, its own private bathroom, a corner Franklin stove, private deck, and French doors opening out to the garden. Although the Garden Room is more spacious, I prefer the country decor of the simple rooms in the main house which are a very good value. In the morning a Continental breakfast with croissants or coffee cake and fresh squeezed orange juice is served. *Directions:* Follow highway 1 north into Mendocino. Turn left at Jackson Street, follow Jackson Street to Kasten Street and turn right.

BLUE HERON INN
Innkeeper: Linda Friedman
390 Kasten Street
Mendocino, CA 95460
Tel: (707) 937-4323
3 bedrooms, 1 with private bathroom
Double from $54 to $90
Open: all year
Credit cards: none accepted
Inappropriate for children

The Headlands Inn is an especially friendly, most attractive small inn located within walking distance of all the pretty shops and fun little restaurants in Mendocino. Like so many of the buildings in town, The Headlands Inn is a New England-style wooden house - a three-story, squarish building with a bay window in front and gables peeking out from the steep roof. A white picket fence encloses the front yard which is usually abloom with flowers in a cheerful English garden. When you enter the small parlor, either Pat or Rod will probably be there to greet you: both are extremely gracious and intent on making your stay a happy one. Steps lead to the upper two floors where four of the bedrooms are located - the fifth is in a detached cottage. Each of these antique-filled guest rooms is exceptionally attractive - none of the heavy Victorian feeling, just light and airy and pretty. There is a fireplace or a Franklin-style stove in each of the bedrooms. My favorite room was Bessie Strauss, a spacious room with a private sitting nook and a large bay window with a view over the road to the bay. But, whatever room you are in, a bountiful breakfast is brought to you on a tray decorated with fresh flowers from the garden - Pat is an exceptional cook and breakfast at the Headlands is a special treat. *Directions:* From San Francisco drive north on highway 101, just past Cloverdale, turn left on highway 128 west to highway 1, and north to Mendocino.

THE HEADLANDS INN
Innkeepers: Pat & Rod Stofle
Howard & Albion Streets, P.O. Box 132
Mendocino, CA 95460
Tel: (707) 937-4431
5 bedrooms with private bathrooms
Double from $85 to $110
Open: all year
Credit cards: none accepted
Children accepted over 16

The Joshua Grindle Inn, located just a short walk from the center of Mendocino, is surrounded by a 2-acre plot of land. A white picket fence encloses the front yard and a walkway leads up to the inn, a most attractive, white clapboard farmhouse which, although architecturally simple, has hints of the Victorian era in the fancy woodwork on the verandah. In the 1879 farmhouse is the guest lounge, a sedate room with old paintings and portraits on the walls, a fireplace, white lace curtains, a trunk for a coffee table and a grand piano tucked in the corner. The light, airy guest rooms have a New England country ambiance enhanced by the owner's early-American antiques and some have their own fireplace. Of the five guest rooms in the main building two overlook the town of Mendocino and the distant ocean. A natural wood cottage just behind the house contains two additional bedrooms. The favorite rooms of many guests are those tucked romantically into the weathered-with-age watertower in the rear garden; especially attractive is Watertower II, a sunny, cozy room on the second floor where the ocean can be glimpsed through the trees. All of the bedrooms are spotlessly maintained, immaculately decorated, have well lighted comfortably arranged sitting areas and private bathrooms. *Directions:* Drive north on highway 1 through Mendocino and turn left on Little Lake Road.

JOSHUA GRINDLE INN
Innkeepers: Jim & Arlene Moorehead
44800 Little Lake Road, P.O. Box 647
Mendocino, CA 95460
Tel: (707) 937-4143
10 bedrooms with private bathrooms
Double from $65 to $100
Open: all year
Credit cards: all major
Children accepted over 10

Most of our selections for Mendocino feature the coastal splendor, but, although not next to the ocean, the Mendocino Farmhouse has its own special qualities. It is located at the end of a narrow lane which weaves through a beautiful redwood glen, crosses a small creek and then opens into a lovely meadow. There, amidst beds of flowers, next to a little duck pond and surrounded by a white picket fence, you will find an appealing tan farmhouse with white trim. Although it appears to be quite old, in reality the inn is newly constructed. Inside the decor is fresh and pretty, with a few antique accents giving it an eclectic style. The breakfast table captures the sunshine in a many-windowed niche overlooking the flower garden. A large family kitchen is located off the living room. Upstairs there are three bedrooms, each sparkling clean and with its own bathroom. The latest additions are suites in the converted barn overlooking the garden, each with a sitting area and a large wood-burning fireplace. One is more rustic in mood, with cedar panelling, antlers over the fireplace and wicker furniture. The other has a bit of a Scandinavian look, with whitewashed pine walls. *Directions:* Just south of Mendocino, turn right off highway 1 on Comptche-Ukiah Road. Go 1 1/2 miles and turn left on Olson Lane - the Mendocino Farmhouse is at the end of the road.

MENDOCINO FARMHOUSE
Innkeepers: Marge & Bud Kamb
Olson Lane, P.O. Box 247
Mendocino, CA 95460
Tel: (707) 937-0241
5 bedrooms with private bathrooms
Double from $70 to $90
Open: all year
Credit cards: none accepted
Children accepted by special arrangement

At first glance The Stanford Inn by the Sea appears to be more like a motel than a country inn, but this is definitely untrue. Joan and Jeff Stanford have done a marvelous job in creating a cozy, sophisticated little hotel within an attractive, but not unusual, two-story, natural wood building. The inn is located across the road from the ocean at the crest of a grassy meadow where a few llamas graze in the blowing grass. The building is cleverly constructed so that every room has a view, either from a private deck or patio. Each guest room has been transformed into a cozy yet elegant little hideaway, with country antiques, many four-poster beds, color television, telephones, bouquets of flowers and either a wood-burning fireplace or stove - with plenty of wood to keep you warm on nippy nights. Everything is fresh and pretty and immaculately clean. The entire operation seems extremely professional and yet has a very personal touch. Each room has a carafe of wine which is kept replenished. In the morning, breakfast is served in the small lounge - most guests take a tray back to their bedroom. Improvements are constantly being introduced: the latest plans are to increase the small breakfast nook into a proper dining area. Joan and Jeff are extremely gracious and devoted to making the guests' stay most pleasant. *Directions:* 1/4 mile south of the village of Mendocino at the intersection of highway 1 and Comptche-Ukiah Road.

THE STANFORD INN BY THE SEA
Innkeepers: Joan & Jeff Stanford
Highway 1 and Comptche-Ukiah Road
Mendocino, CA 95460
Tel: (707) 937-5615
25 bedrooms with private bathrooms
Double from $120 to $160
Open: all year
Credit cards: all major
Children accepted

Gene and Ann Swett converted their family home into what continues to be one of the very nicest country inns in California. Their home is a most attractive Tudor-style house shaded by giant oak trees in an acre of wooded gardens full of colorful begonias, fuchsias, rhododendrons and lush ferns in a quiet Monterey suburb. Everything is beautifully tended, giving the grounds a parklike appearance. The inside of the house is an oasis of gentility and tranquility where everything is done with the comfort of the guest in mind. Most of the bedrooms in the main house, cottage and carriage house have fireplaces, all are beautifully decorated and thoughtfully appointed. The library stands out as a particularly memorable bedroom with its book-lined walls, cozy fireplace and private balcony overlooking the garden. A refrigerator is kept stocked with complimentary beverages, and juices and hot beverages are always available. In an evening the Swetts join their guests for wine and cheese in the living room. They are especially gracious hosts, adding great warmth and professionalism to their little inn. Breakfast is served at the long oak table in the dining room or brought to your room on a tray. This is certainly the place for a romantic getaway. *Directions:* Travelling south on highway 1 take the Soledad/Munras exit, cross Munras Avenue, then go right on Pacific Street: Martin Street is on your left in a little over half a mile.

OLD MONTEREY INN
Innkeepers: Gene & Ann Swett
500 Martin Street
Monterey, CA 93940
Tel: (408) 375-8284
10 bedrooms with private bathrooms
Double from $135 to $195
Open: all year
Credit cards: none accepted
Children accepted over 14

The Inn at Morro Bay has a superb setting in a wooded park which slopes down to the waterfront. The layout is hotel-like, with strips of lowrise buildings in a garden setting, but the impression is of an attractive New England coastal town. The wooden buildings are painted a weathered driftwood gray, accented with white porches, banisters and shutters. Flowers are everywhere, even lining the parking lot. A pretty swimming pool is conveniently placed between the buildings. The wing of rooms nearest the harbor enjoys unobstructed bay views. The lobby, reception lounge and the award-winning restaurant share one building and are formal and somewhat commerical looking. More outstanding than the public rooms are the bedrooms: each is prettily decorated in a French country look with reproduction armoires, brass beds and pretty floral fabrics. Many also have a fireplace. Even the least expensive rooms have the same appealing decor and quiet elegance. This is one of the few inns in our guide which is not owner-managed, but the staff is extremely friendly. We were pleased to discover The Inn at Morro Bay since we wanted to find a nice place to stay on this section of the coast which would accept children. Happily, although not your typical small county inn, it is a most acceptable choice. *Directions:* Drive south through town on Main Street and, at the entrance to the park, you see the inn on your right.

THE INN AT MORRO BAY
Innkeeper: Paul Nakamura
19 Country Club Drive
Morro Bay, CA 93442
Tel: (805) 772-5651 or (800) 321-9566
98 bedrooms with private bathrooms
Double from $95 to $235
Open: all year
Credit cards: all major
Children accepted

At long last we are going to fulfill a dream of many years: opening our own country inn. We are thrilled with the location - a spectacular piece of property bordered by towering, wind-swept Cypress trees, looking out over acres of state park to the ocean. From the inn one can walk to the secluded stretch of beach or wind through the forest on the path that traces the ocean bluffs to visit the Marine Reserve. Moss Beach is located on the coast south of San Francisco, two miles north of the scenic harbor town of Princeton with its delightful restaurants and seven miles north of Half Moon Bay. Public rooms will be furnished with antiques lovingly collected over the past fifteen years with an inn in mind. A large fireplace will warm the cozy living room - library, an inviting place to settle after an ocean walk or an invigorating bike ride in the brisk salt air. Each spacious bedroom will be its own private haven with a queen-sized bed, comfortable sitting area, fireplace and French windows opening onto views of the beautiful property. Our inn will be a romantic oasis in which to relax, be pampered and enjoy a few quiet days near the grandeur of the sea. *Directions:* From San Francisco, take highway 280 or 101 south and then travel west on highway 92. When 92 deadends at highway 1, travel north seven miles to Moss Beach. Turn left on Cypress Avenue. (*Estimated opening late 1990)*

SEAL COVE INN
Innkeepers: Karen (Brown) & Rick Herbert
Cypress Avenue
Moss Beach, CA 94038
Tel: (415) 342-9117
10 bedrooms with private bathrooms
Conference facilities for small groups
Double from $125
Open: all year
Credit cards: all major
Children accepted

The Pelican Inn is a wonderful re-creation of a cozy English tavern with a few attractive guest rooms tucked upstairs. Your host, Barry Stock (from Devon), has a delightful British accent that adds to the impression that you must be in England. Wide wood-planked floors, an appealing small bar (with dart board), low beamed ceilings, a giant fireplace with priest hole (secret hiding place), a cozy little guest lounge and a dining room with trestle tables complete the first floor scene. Besides the large indoor dining room, there is also a trellised patio where guests can have snacks or dine (in the evenings the candle-lit tables are set with linens). And dining is a treat: the menu features such English dishes as succulent bangers, cottage pie, prime rib and rack of lamb. Upstairs there are seven cozy bedrooms where the English motif is carried out with heavily draped half-tester beds, Oriental carpets, a decanter of sherry and fresh flowers. You might not want to step out of this little oasis, but the location of the Pelican Inn is fabulous. Only a few minutes' drive from the giant redwood grove at Muir Woods, the Pelican Inn is located a short walk from the ocean, nestled among pines and alders, honeysuckle and jasmine. Make reservations at least six months in advance for weekends. *Directions:* From highway 101, take the Stinson Beach highway 1 exit. Turn left at Muir Beach and the inn is on your right.

PELICAN INN
Innkeeper: Barry Stock
Muir Beach, CA 94965
Tel: (415) 383-6000
7 Bedrooms with private bathrooms
Double from $105 to $130
Open: all year
Credit cards: MC, VS
Children accepted

"Gold in them thar hills" enticed fortune seekers to Murphys by the legion. The gold boom passed and Murphys was left to sleep under its locust and elm trees until tourists discovered its beauty and slower pace of life. A few old stone buildings survive, one of which contains the Old Timers' Museum filled with pioneer and Gold Rush regalia. Just a few steps away is Dunbar House, 1880, a handsome inn with a wrap-around porch where guests can sit and sip gold-country wine or enjoy a refreshing glass of lemonade. Bob and Barbara's pride in their small inn is apparent - they have lavished their time and attention on making it extremely comfortable. With just five guest rooms, the atmosphere is very cozy. The Sequoia room, downstairs at the front of the house, has a queen-size bed and a clawfoot tub set before a wood stove. The Cedar room, just off the downstairs parlor, has a delightful, sun-filled porch perfect for a private breakfast. Upstairs are two additional pretty bedrooms. While you are out at dinner your bed will be turned down and chocolates placed on your pillow. Breakfast includes juice spritzer, fresh fruit, muffins, turnovers, an egg dish and a hot beverage - during the summer it is served outside in the garden. *Directions:* From the San Francisco area take highway 580 to highway 99 north to highway 4 east, drive through Angels Camp and on towards Arnold. Murphys is 9 miles east of Angels Camp.

DUNBAR HOUSE, 1880
Innkeepers: Bob & Barbara Costa
271 Jones Street, P.O. Box 1375
Murphys, CA 95247
Tel: (209) 728-2897
5 bedrooms with private bathrooms
Double from $70 to $75
Open: all year
Credit cards: MC, VS
Children accepted over 10

La Residence is an inn that has grown around the Mansion, a beautiful Gothic revival home built in the 1870s as a farmhouse to accommodate a large family by Harry Parker, a riverboat pilot from New Orleans. In later years additions more Victorian in style changed the appearance of the home. Nine rooms are housed in the original mansion and are dramatic in their decor which blends well with the grand feeling of the home. Rooms vary from cozy, top-floor rooms tucked under slanted ceilings to spacious and elegant accommodations with fireplaces on the first floor. The eleven rooms in the newly constructed Cabernet Hall, shingled and built in the style of a French barn, are beautifully designed and commodious, each enjoying a private bath, fireplace and French doors that open onto a private patio or balcony. These bedrooms are handsomely decorated with pine antiques imported from France and England and Laura Ashley prints. Breakfast is served in the Cabernet Hall's lovely dining room with tables set before a blazing fire. Between the Mansion and the Cabernet Hall are a swimming pool and jacuzzi spa. The excellence of the inn reflects the expertise and talents contributed by the partners who share in the management. *Directions:* North of Napa, after the cross-street Salvador, turn right onto a frontage road (no name) which winds back south to the inn.

LA RESIDENCE
Innkeepers: David Jackson & Craig Claussen
4066 St Helena Highway
Napa, CA 94558
Tel: (707) 253-0337
20 bedrooms, 18 with private bathrooms
Double from $65 to $150
Open: all year
Credit cards: MC, VS
Children accepted

High on the hillside looking out over green lawns to distant villas and sprawling acreage of planted vineyards, Oakville Ranch is expensive, unique and affords a very private, romantic and exclusive getaway. Built as a winery in 1904, it was converted to a private home at the time of prohibition. Just over a decade ago it was purchased with plans to use it as a vacation home and to rent rooms to overnight guests. Of the twelve marvelous rooms originally intended for rental, recent codes have restricted the number to three incredible suites. Off the entry on the first floor, the enormous Chardonnay suite bridges what was once the gap between two buildings. It has an enormous king canopy bed sitting on a platform in the center of the room, a bath with a large jacuzzi tub and a shower that backs into the original stone walls. Upstairs, two spacious rooms divide the width of the building and open up with French doors onto a shared but expansive deck. A downstairs country kitchen with a well stocked refrigerator and open bar are available to guests without charge. Hors d'oeuvres are served in the afternoon and enjoyed with the ranch's own bottled chardonnay. *Directions:* After Oakville Cross Road, travelling north on the Silverado Trail, watch for 7781 posted with other addresses and turn right on a private road that winds a mile or so up to the security gates.

OAKVILLE RANCH
Innkeeper: Cindy Lindquist
7781 Silverado Trail
Napa, CA 94558
Tel: (707) 944-8612
3 suites with private bathrooms
Double from $250 to $300
Open: all year
Credit cards: none accepted
Inappropriate for children

CLOSED

When gold was discoverea, Nevada City became an affluent boom town. It remains prosperous-looking, its beautifully restored downtown area full of tempting restaurants and inviting shops. Just beyond Broad Street's shopping district, enclosed within a mature garden of long rolling lawns and tidy bushes, sits Grandmere's Inn, a stately Colonial Revival home built for Aaron Sargant, a U.S. Congressman and his suffragette wife, Ellen. Ellen's friend, Susan B. Anthony, often stayed here and Aaron authored the bill that eventually gave women the right to vote. How appropriate that Grandmere's be owned and operated by a woman, your innkeeper, Annette Meade. The five upstairs rooms are named after her three children, Joseph, John and Devon, and her parents, Nana and Papa. Annette has a tremendous knack for putting things together with great flair. Pale gray is the dominant color although each bedroom has its own personality. A downstairs suite has a private garden entry and can accommodate children travelling with their parents. In the morning the aroma of coffee fills the air and at 9:00AM the sideboard is loaded with sliced fruits, breakfast casseroles, muffins and croissants. Portions are bountiful and there is no need to worry about lunch. *Directions:* From the San Francisco area take the I 80 to the 49 north 29 miles to Nevada City, exit at Broad Street and turn left up the main street of the town.

GRANDMERE'S
Innkeeper: Annette Meade
449 Broad Street
Nevada City, CA 95959
Tel: (916) 265-4660
6 bedrooms with private bathrooms
Double from $85 to $125
Open: all year
Credit cards: MC, VS
Children accepted in the downstairs suite

It was fun to discover The Doryman's Inn, a sophisticated, elaborately decorated small hotel next to the Newport Beach Pier. This is not a sophisticated location: just across the street, next to the old wooden wharf, the fishermen still go to sea every day (as they have for 100 years) in their brightly painted dories and return to sell their catch from the back of the boats. For beach buffs, the sand stretches for miles to the entrance to Balboa Harbor. The hotel entry is quite discreet: just a tiny hall where an elevator takes you up to the reception area - the inn is located above the Rex Restaurant, a dining establishment famous for its seafood. When you step off the elevator you are immersed in the romantic ambiance of the Victorian era with elaborate panelling, reproduction gas lamps, dark wallpaper and busy floral carpeting. The bedrooms open off the long hallway which is lit with skylights and graced by baskets of hanging ferns. Each of the bedrooms is elaborately decorated with splendid antique beds, fireplaces, and Italian-marble sunken bathtubs. No expense was spared - and it shows. In the morning a light breakfast of fresh pastries, seasonal fruits, yoghurts and assorted cheeses is served buffet-style in the small dining room or out on the patio. *Directions:* Take highway 5 west toward Newport Beach and follow the signs to the Newport Pier: the hotel is across the street.

DORYMAN'S INN
Innkeeper: Michael Sorrell
2102 West Ocean Front
Newport Beach, CA 92663
Tel: (714) 675-7300
10 bedrooms with private bathrooms
Double from $135 to $275
Open: all year
Credit cards: all major
Inappropriate for children

Sandwiched between the busier resorts of Monterey and Carmel, Pacific Grove has managed to avoid much of their more touristy ambiance and retains the air of being an inviting Victorian summer retreat. And the Gosby House is a perfect place to retreat to, with certainly a lot more fun and frolic than in days gone by when it was the summer home of a stern Methodist family. While the decor is decidedly Victorian in flavor, it has been done with such whimsy and fun that all formal stuffiness has been dispelled: a glass-fronted cabinet in the dining room is filled with antique dolls and teddy bears are rakishly posed on each bed. The bedrooms are scattered upstairs and down, some have garden entrances and several occupy an adjacent clapboard house tucked behind the pretty garden. Over half the bedrooms have fireplaces and all but two have luxuriously appointed bathrooms. Each room is appealingly decorated in soft colors and many benefit from the romantic touch of antique beds. Before you venture out for dinner, enjoy hors d'oeuvres, wine and sherry in the living room. When you return, your bed will be turned down and a rose and chocolates placed on your pillow - such a sweet way to end the day. *Directions:* Take highway 1 to highway 68 west to Pacific Grove. Continue on Forest Avenue to Lighthouse Avenue, turn left and go three blocks to the inn.

GOSBY HOUSE
Innkeeper: Kelly Short
643 Lighthouse Avenue
Pacific Grove, CA 93950
Tel: (408) 375-1287
22 bedrooms, 20 with private bathrooms
Double from $85 to $125
Open: all year
Credit cards: all major
Children accepted in annex rooms

The Green Gables Inn is sensationally positioned overlooking Monterey Bay. This romantic, half-timbered, Queen Anne-style mansion with many interesting dormers is as inviting inside as out. The living room and dining room have comfortable arrangements of sofas and chairs placed to maximize your enjoyment of the view. Upstairs many of the bedrooms, set under steeply slanting beamed ceilings with romantic diamond-paned casement windows, offer ocean views. While the Garret room does not have an ocean view, it is the coziest of hideaways. All but one of the upstairs bedrooms share a bathroom. The ground floor suite has a sitting room and fireplace. The more modern rooms in the adjacent carriage house all have fireplaces, sitting areas and private bathrooms. While a guest at The Green Gables Inn you will certainly not perish from hunger or thirst - beverages are available all day, goodies readily available in the cookie jar, and wine and hors d'oeuvres appear in the evening. Breakfast, too, is no disappointment: a hearty buffet of fruit, homemade breads and a hot egg dish. *Directions:* From highway 1 take the Pacific Grove - Del Monte exit. As you go through the tunnel Del Monte becomes Lighthouse Avenue which you follow into Pacific Grove. Go right one block and you are on Ocean View Boulevard and the inn is on the corner at Fifth Street.

THE GREEN GABLES INN
Innkeeper: Claudia Long
104 Fifth Street
Pacific Grove, CA 93950
Tel: (408) 375-2095
11 bedrooms, 7 with private bathrooms
Double from $95 to $135
Open: all year
Credit cards: all major
Children accepted over 12

Guests of The House of Seven Gables Inn are afforded a breathtaking outlook across Monterey Bay. This sunny, yellow Victorian house and its guest cottages are perfectly positioned on a corner lot, and angled so that a great many of the bedrooms and the public rooms have unobstructed ocean views. Owned by Nora and Jon Flatley, the inn is by and large managed by their children Susan, Fred and Ed. You enter into a large living room decorated with very ornate, formal European furnishings complemented by lots of very fussy accessories and fixtures: fancy chandeliers, ornate Oriental rugs and frilly curtains, such as are found in the more formal hotels of Europe. Just off the living room is the dining room which opens onto a sun porch where you can choose between watching television or the ocean. Or you can opt for ocean vistas from one of the inn's four sheltered patios. Breakfast is a sit-down affair, the table elegantly set with china and fine linen. For those who love to be out in the fresh air, just across the street a many-mile pathway parallels the bay, perfect for bicycling, walking or jogging. Cannery Row and the aquarium are along this path. *Directions:* From highway 1 take the Pacific Grove - Del Monte exit. As you go through the tunnel Del Monte becomes Lighthouse Avenue which you follow into Pacific Grove. Go right one block and you are on Ocean View Boulevard.

THE HOUSE OF SEVEN GABLES INN
Innkeepers: The Flatley Family
555 Ocean View Blvd
Pacific Grove, CA 93950
Tel: (408) 372-4341
14 bedrooms with private bathrooms
Double from $85 to $155
Open: all year
Credit cards: none accepted
Inappropriate for children

The Casa Cody is a moderately-priced hotel in the heart of Palm Springs which, although nothing fancy, stands out like a gem amongst its neighbors. Upon first glance the inn appears to be an old-fashioned motel-style establishment with a pool in the central courtyard and rooms in a U shape surrounding it. And indeed it is an old hotel - the second oldest in Palm Springs. It had fallen into a state of disrepair until recently when it was bought by Therese Hayes (who is French) and Frank Tysen (who is Dutch). Therese showed me photos of what they faced when buying the hotel - it looked quite hopeless. But after a year of hard work and lots of imagination the hotel has blossomed into a very pleasant place to stay. There is a nice choice of types of accommodations, ranging from a studio to a two-bedroom, two-bath unit. Units all have kitchens and fireplaces. The interior decor exudes a fresh, clean look that Therese describes as "Santa Fe with a touch of French". The colors are pretty pastels and the furniture handmade. During the week, coffee is served each morning on the patio and on weekends pastries are also offered to the guests. The Casa Cody cannot accept children on weekends, but, if you call in advance, they are usually welcome mid-week. *Directions:* Drive through Palm Springs south on Palm Canyon Drive, turn right on Tahquitz-McCallum Road for two blocks and left on Cahuilla Road.

CASA CODY
Innkeepers: Therese Hayes & Frank Tysen
175 South Cahuilla Road
Palm Springs, CA 92262
Tel: (619) 320-9346
10 suites with private bathrooms
Double from $95 to $120
Open: all year
Credit cards: all major
Children accepted mid-week

As you enter the large wrought iron gates of the Ingleside Inn, you have the impression of being the guest on a private estate. This is not surprising, since the Ingleside Inn was once the home of the Humphrey Birge family, manufacturers of the Pierce Arrow automobile. Although the hotel is located in the heart of Palm Springs it is an oasis of tranquility. The parklike grounds are surrounded by a high adobe wall and the San Jacinto Mountains rise steeply behind the hotel, forming a dramatic background. A pretty pool and gazebo highlight the front lawn of the hotel. Some of the guest rooms open off an inner courtyard, while others are nestled in nearby cottages. Each room is individually decorated and features antiques, and all have whirlpool tubs and refrigerators stocked with complimentary light snacks: many have wood-burning fireplaces. Breakfast is served either on the verandah, poolside, or on your private patio. The owner of Ingleside Inn, Melvyn Haber, also owns one of the famous restaurants in Palm Springs, appropriately called "Melvyn's", which is located next to the lobby. In the evening the restaurant traffic intrudes somewhat upon the solitude, but it is wonderfully convenient to have such an excellent restaurant so close at hand. *Directions:* Drive through Palm Springs south on Palm Canyon Drive and turn right on Ramon Road. You see the inn on your right.

INGLESIDE INN
Innkeeper: Babs Rosen
200 West Ramon Road
Palm Springs, CA 92262
Tel: (619) 325-0046
29 bedrooms with private bathrooms
Double from $95 to $225
Open: all year
Credit cards: all major
Inappropriate for children

Before opening the Villa Royale, Chuck Murawski, one of the owners, was a Broadway set designer - a fact readily apparent when you see the imaginative decor throughout this small inn. The overall theme is romantic Spanish, with softly splashing fountains, walls draped in bougainvillea, decorative tile work, secluded little nooks, columned arcades, overhanging tiled roofs and meandering paths. But it is the guest rooms which are very special: not only do many have their own wood-burning fireplaces and private spas, but each accommodation represents a country, so you can choose your room to blend with your mood, with such options in decor as Irish, English, Moorish, Swiss, Italian, German, Spanish, Dutch and Greek. There are 3 1/2 acres of walled oasis in which the rooms are cleverly arranged for maximum privacy around several interior courtyards. One courtyard has a swimming pool with a nearby terrace where tables are set for lunch or snacks. Dinner is served in a most attractive dining room whose decor is very European-countryside. The Villa Royale is a short distance from the center of town - a bit far to walk, but bicycles are conveniently at hand next to the office for guests to use for shopping or sightseeing. *Directions:* Drive south through Palm Springs on Palm Canyon Drive and just a couple of blocks after the road makes a bend to the left and becomes East Palm Canyon Drive, turn left on Indian Trail.

VILLA ROYALE
Innkeepers: Charles Murawski & Robert Lee
1620 Indian Trail
Palm Springs, CA 92264
Tel: (619) 327-2314
31 bedrooms with private bathrooms
Double from $75 to $145
Open: all year
Credit cards: all major
Inappropriate for children

Palo Alto, home to famous Stanford University, is an attractive town filled with art galleries, gift shops, smart boutiques and fun restaurants. Just one block from the town's main street (University Avenue), Susan and Maxwell have converted a beautiful old Victorian into a most attractive, well-run inn. The guest rooms are located both in the main house and in a new addition in the garden. All of the guest rooms are individually decorated with great charm and taste. The beds, most four-poster or canopy-style, are fine quality antique reproductions with excellent mattresses. Susan personally chose the furniture and fabrics throughout the inn and planned each room. She even sewed the duvet covers for the down comforters, curtains, dust ruffles and fancy pillows. The garden is very pretty with nearly 500 varieties of plants, many of them brought from England and lovingly planted in California. To start each day, a Continental breakfast is brought to each room on a tray. In the evening, guests congregate in the lounge for complimentary sherry or port. This is a very lovely little inn with a great bonus of excellent management: Susan is not only a gracious hostess, but also an excellent housekeeper - everything is spotlessly clean. *Directions:* Driving south from San Francisco on highway 101 take the University Avenue (Palo Alto) exit west then turn right at Middlefield and left on Lytton.

THE VICTORIAN ON LYTTON
Innkeeper: Susan Hall
555 Lytton Avenue
Palo Alto, CA 94301
Tel: (415) 322-8555
10 bedrooms with private bathrooms
Double from $90 to $135
Open: all year
Credit cards: all major
Children accepted over 15

The Thirty-nine Cypress is not old; it is not brimming with antiques; it is not decorator-perfect; it is not cutesy country: but it radiates warmth. A winding cobbled path leads through a profusion of happy flowers to the entry of the weathered-wood low building which blends into the landscape. The main room features a large fireplace encased with well-worn books. Facing the fireplace a comfortable sofa invites you to snuggle down with a good book and cup of tea. The country-style kitchen shows all the touches of someone who loves to cook. A patio leads out to the back where an idyllic view spreads before you with cattle grazing in the fields below. There are only three bedrooms: two have a private washbasin and toilet plus an outdoor nook with a shower stall with a terry cloth robe hanging conveniently near. The third bedroom has a bathroom off the hallway and if guests feel uncomfortable showering outdoors, they can use this bathroom's shower. Julia calls the furnishings "Family-Illinois" since most came with her when she moved out to California. There is no particular style, but everything is combined to exude an appealing welcome: nothing contrived nor stiff - the entire atmosphere says stay, relax, and forget the cares of the real world. *Directions:* Drive north through town on highway 1: after the road makes a right turn, go left on Mesa. Drive for about a mile and turn right on Cypress.

THIRTY-NINE CYPRESS
Innkeeper: Julia Bartlett
39 Cypress
Point Reyes Station, CA 94956
Tel: (415) 663-1709
3 bedrooms, 2 with private bathrooms
Double from $85 to $95
Open: all year except Christmas
Credit cards: none accepted
Inappropriate for small children

The East Brother Light Station, snugly sitting on its own tiny island, dates back to 1873 when it was built to guide ships through a 2-mile wide strait connecting San Francisco Bay and San Pablo Bay. Adjoining the tower beacon, a small house with gingerbread trim was built for the lightkeepers and their families. This nostalgic lighthouse was doomed for destruction: when a group of concerned citizens banded together, raised the funds and saved it. (Among them, Walter Fanning, who spent many happy hours at the East Brother Light Station as a boy when his grandfather was the lighthouse keeper.) Today, a few lucky guests enjoy the island in far more luxurious circumstances than the keepers of old. Guests are brought by boat in the afternoon, treated to a delicious five-course dinner, then lulled to sleep by the sound of fog-horns. There are four guest rooms, not large and luxurious, but pleasantly decorated with antiques and and all with a view of the bay. The innkeepers, Linda and Leigh Hurley, live on the island with their little daughter. Leigh does the cooking and Linda graciously tends to the needs of the guests. Because all the water is caught from the rain (and it has recently been very dry) only guests staying more than one night may use the showers. *Directions:* Call the inn for details on the time to meet the boat and how to get to the pier. Point Richmond is on the Richmond side of the Richmond-San Raphael Bridge.

EAST BROTHER LIGHT STATION
Innkeepers: Linda & Leigh Hurley
117 Park Place
Point Richmond, CA 94801
Tel: (415) 278-6429
4 bedrooms, 2 with private bathrooms
Double $285 (includes breakfast & dinner)
Open: all year, Thursday through Sunday nights
Credit cards: none accepted
Inappropriate for children

Quincy is a placid town in the High Sierras with the kind of pace of life that city dwellers long for. Chuck and Dianna left farming in Bakersfield to move here, bought a rambling, rundown Victorian house, spent many hours of love and caring in fixing it up and became innkeepers. The Feather Bed was built as a family home in 1893, but at some point its internal staircase to the bedrooms was removed and it became a small apartment/boarding house with narrow wooden staircases leading up the side of the house to the bedchambers. The same arrangement exists today, but now the bedrooms are prettily papered and each also has the convenience of a spotlessly clean private bathroom. The furnishings are very simple and the slanting ceilings give a snug coziness. (Please note that there is no air conditioning so it can be hot in summer - in winter the rooms are warmed by wall heaters.) At the back of the house the gardener's cottage has a sitting area and French windows that open up to a small private patio. Also at the back of the house is a small outdoor theatre where old-fashioned melodramas are performed during the summer. Chuck prides himself on his breakfasts, serving them outside on the patio in the summer or in the dining room during the winter. *Directions:* Take I 80 to Truckee where you turn north on highway 89-70 for the 75-mile drive to Quincy: the Feather Bed is behind the courthouse.

THE FEATHER BED
Innkeepers: Chuck & Dianna Goubert
542 Jackson Street
Quincy, CA 95971
Tel: (916) 283-0102
7 bedrooms with private bathrooms
Double from $55 to $75
Open: all year
Credit cards: all major
Children accepted over 12

The known history of the Rancho Santa Fe property dates back to 1845 when an 8,842 acre land grant was given to Juan Maria Osuna. Then in 1906 the Santa Fe Railroad purchased the land grant, changed the name to Rancho Santa Fe and planted about three million eucalyptus seedlings with the idea of growing wood for railroad ties. The project failed: the wood was not appropriate. So the railroad decided instead to develop a planned community and built a lovely Spanish-style guest house for prospective home buyers. This became the nucleus for what is now the Inn at Rancho Santa Fe and houses the lounges, dining rooms, offices and a few of the guest rooms. The lounge is extremely appealing, like a cozy living room in a private home, with a large fireplace, comfortable seating, impressive floral arrangements and a roaring fire. The dining rooms are more "hotel-like" in ambiance. The bedrooms, most tucked away in cottages scattered throughout the property, are attractively decorated with traditional fabrics and furnishings and many have fireplaces. The grounds are lovely, filled with flowers and shaded by fragrant eucalyptus trees. The inn's greatest asset is the Royce family, who own the hotel and give what first appears to be a slick commerical resort, the warmth and friendliness of a small inn. *Directions:* From San Diego go north for 25 miles on highway 5 and take the Lomas Santa Fe Drive turnoff. The inn is in 6 miles.

INN AT RANCHO SANTA FE
Innkeeper: Daniel L. Royce
Linea del Ciele at Paseo Delicias
Rancho Santa Fe, CA 92067
Tel: (619) 756-1131
75 bedrooms with private bathrooms
Double from $90 to $165 (without breakfast)
Open: all year
Credit cards: all major
Children accepted

The Ink House is a beautiful landmark on highway 29 at the corner of Whitehall Lane. It is a stunning, dark brown, two-story building, trimmed in crisp white with an encircling porch, crowned by an enclosed observatory built by Supervisor T. H. Ink in 1884. Quite impressive, the project was announced in the local paper as "a dwelling built that is as imposing in its appearance as it is elaborate in finish and roominess". In recent decades the Ink House has been home to the Clark family: Lois and George raised five children and, once their rooms were vacated, were among the first in the valley to open their home to overnight guests and establish themselves in the innkeeping business. Lois is your hostess and, although she has had more than a decade to perfect her hospitality, time was not necessary to instill what comes naturally to her - a warm, genuine caring for her guests. The bedrooms are at the top of a long, steep flight of stairs. Each room, named for the Clark women (Teresa, Marilyne, Sheilah and Lois), has its own private bath and is decorated with antique beds set on handsome, wood-planked floors. The third-floor observatory, painted white and decorated with white wicker furniture, is enclosed on four sides by stained glass windows (from Scotland) and looks out to 360 degrees of unobstructed views of the valley. *Directions:* 16 miles north of Napa on highway 29 at Whitehall Lane.

INK HOUSE
Innkeeper: Lois Clark
1575 St Helena Highway
St Helena, CA 94574
Tel: (707) 963-3890
4 bedrooms with private bathrooms
Double from $80 to $110
Open: all year
Credit cards: none accepted
Inappropriate for children

On 256 sprawling acres, Meadowood, an attractive complex of sand-gray gabled wooden buildings, is a resort community in a secluded, quiet valley sheltered by towering ponderosa pines and Douglas firs. Wooded areas open up to a golf course, two croquet courts and numerous tennis courts. Centrally located, the clubhouse, a rambling, three-story structure that overlooks the croquet lawn and golf course, houses an excellent restaurant, the Starmont, the less formal Fairway Grill and Bar, shops, meeting rooms, an inviting lodge room with a wonderful fieldstone fireplace and thirteen guest rooms. Other rooms are found in clusters of lodges scattered about the property. The atmosphere, relaxed, informal, unpretentious, is accurately described as "California casual". Although expensive, the accommodations are luxuriously appointed and attractively furnished, reflecting an incredible attention to detail. Concern for a guest's comfort and satisfaction is foremost and service is carried out with a friendly and professional flair. Meadowood is a luxurious resort with every amenity and with a most caring friendly staff. *Directions:* From St Helena take Pope Street east from highway 29 to the Silverado Trail, cross the Silverado Trail, a slight jog to the left and follow Howell Mountain Road and Meadowood signs.

MEADOWOOD RESORT HOTEL
Innkeeper: Maurice Nayrolles
900 Meadowood Lane
St Helena, CA 94574
Tel: (707) 963-3646
70 bedrooms with private bathrooms
Double from $210 to $300
Open: all year
Credit cards: all major
Children accepted

With an entry tucked off a small shopping arcade on St Helena's delightful main street, the Hotel St Helena affords an ideal location for those who want to stay within walking distance of shops and a wide range of interesting restaurants. The attractive lobby, decorated in rich tones of burgundy, mauve and brown, sets an inviting ambiance that is carried through to the decor in the bedrooms. A few steps up off the lobby is an extremely cozy wine bar whose intimate tables are set against rose-colored walls and dressed with pink cloths. Here you can sample by the glass from over thirty varieties of Napa Valley wines and accompany your tasting with tempting appetizers or cheese plates. In addition, the wine bar serves a large selection of imported beers, coffees and teas. A Continental breakfast of scones, muffins, fresh fruit and hot beverages is also served in the wine bar and on sunny days you can carry a tray out into the lovely garden courtyard. The hotel's 17 bedrooms are located up a narrow flight of stairs decorated with attractive prints on the walls. While the guestrooms are on the small side, most have private bathrooms and all are delightfully decorated and furnished with Victorian antiques including some brass headboards and bent willow furniture. *Directions:* Located on the west side of Main Street in downtown St Helena.

HOTEL ST HELENA
Innkeeper: Athena Martin
1309 Main Street
St. Helena, CA 94574
Tel: (707) 963-4388
17 bedrooms, 14 with private bathrooms
Double from $75 to $125
Open: all year
Credit cards: all major
Inappropriate for children

The Wine Country Inn is a new complex of buildings built of wood and stone, fashioned after the inns of New England, settled on a low hillside and surrounded by acres of vineyards. The inn has twenty-five rooms which have been oriented to enjoy the tranquil and scenic setting: fifteen rooms are housed in the main building, six in the Brandy Barn and four in the Hastings House. Many of the rooms have private patios, balconies and fireplaces that are useable mid-October to mid-April. Each room has its own bath and is individually decorated with country furnishings, unique in its appeal and character. Many of the quilts were handmade by the owners. Although our room was not completely buffered from the sounds next door, the inn is praised for its peaceful setting and knowledgeable and friendly staff. Public areas include a lovely lobby that opens onto a large expanse of deck and a pool on the terraced hillside bounded by a patio and colorful gardens. *Directions:* Two miles north of St Helena on highway 29 turn right onto Lodi Lane. The Wine Country Inn is in 1/4 mile on the left.

THE WINE COUNTRY INN
Innkeeper: Jim Smith
1152 Lodi Lane
St Helena, CA 94574
Tel: (707) 963-7077
25 bedrooms with private bathrooms
Double from $93 to $161
Open: all year
Credit cards: MC, VS
Children accepted over 12

Britt House, built lavishly in 1887 as a family home for Eugene Britt, is a dramatic and ornate Victorian located just a few blocks from the San Diego Zoo. Although only one room has a private bath, Britt House offers some of the best bed and breakfast accommodation in the city. It is professionally managed by Daun Martin who seems to anticipate her guests' every need and graciously attempts to accommodate any special requests. Rooms enjoy high ceilings, hand-worked oak interiors, intricate scrolling and lovely molding. Off the entry a magnificent stairway is bathed in light, backed by two stories of stained glass windows. Bedrooms are found on each level and in a separate, one-bedroom cottage. Throughout, the decor is in keeping with the atmosphere of this wonderful old home: antiques are placed in abundance and copies of Victorian wallpapers add dramatic color to many of the rooms. Rooms are supplied with fresh fruit, cookies, baskets of towels and soaps, bathrobes and fresh flowers. Daun is present each morning to personally serve her guests a gourmet breakfast, either in their room or the parlor. Guests are welcomed to the inn with a bounty of cakes, cookies, breads, tea and lemonade. The inn has several resident pets - a dog, a bird and three cats. *Directions:* Turn east on Washington Street off highway 5 to 4th Avenue. Turn right on 4th and go about 2 miles to Maple.

BRITT HOUSE
Innkeeper: Daun Martin
406 Maple Street
San Diego, CA 92103
Tel: (619) 234-2926
10 bedrooms, 1 with private bathroom
Double from $85 to $105
Open: all year
Credit cards: all major
Children accepted

Cresting the top of a lovely, quiet pedestrian street just a few blocks from Old Town, the Heritage Park Bed & Breakfast, a beautifully restored Queen Anne mansion, shares 7 acres of English gardens with 6 other lovely restored Victorians. Each gingerbread house was relocated from downtown to create this charming hillock village of interesting shops, museums and inn. Very Victorian in its decor, the Heritage Park Bed & Breakfast offers the romantic some lovely accommodation. With lots of lace, patterned wallpapers, antique furnishings and knickknacks such as cookie cutters, lace-up boots, antique clothes and potpourri hearts dressing every nook and corner, the decor is fussy, almost museum-like. You enter off the street into a parlor hung with deep-red velvet curtains. A chalkboard tells guests of the film classic to be shown that evening accompanied by wine cider and popcorn. The Heritage Park has nine rooms, some of which enjoy views over the city and bay, and fireplaces or cozy nooks tucked into the turrets. Although not all have private baths, each room is set with a table and two chairs where you can enjoy a gourmet breakfast or a prearranged candlelight dinner. *Directions:* From Los Angeles follow interstate 5 south to the Old Town Avenue exit, then go left on San Diego Avenue. At Harney, turn right: it leads into the park with plenty of off-street parking just below the hotel.

HERITAGE PARK BED & BREAKFAST
Innkeeper: Lori Chandler
2470 Heritage Park Row
San Diego, CA 92110
Tel: (619) 295-7088
9 bedrooms, 3 with private bathrooms
Double from $75 to $115
Open: all year
Credit cards: MC, VS
Children accepted over 14

Archbishops Mansion is located on Alamo Square in an historic Victorian district of the city saved from fires after the 1906 San Francisco earthquake, just six blocks from the Opera House. Impressive in structure as well as in its role in San Francisco's history, the mansion since its construction in 1904 has served as the residence for three Archbishops and as a Catholic boys' school. The careful and artful supervision of Jonathan Shannon and Jeffrey Ross has now transformed it into a small luxury-class hotel. Extravagant furnishings have been selected to match the sophisticated elegance of the building. Crystal chandeliers illuminate the high, intricately sculpted ceilings, marble encases many of the fourteen working fireplaces and, of the fifteen guest rooms, even the smallest is large by standard hotel offerings. A grand staircase winds up three stories to the bedrooms, exposed to a large stained glass skylight. Each room is named for an opera whose theme stages a mood for the decor. Copies of the libretto are left in each room. In the ornate parlor complimentary wine is served accompanied by piano selections played on a 1904 Bechstein once owned by Noel Coward. An especially elegant Continental breakfast is brought to your room in a French picnic basket. *Directions:* From the south take 101 to Fell Street, travel 5 blocks, and then turn right onto Steiner: continue 3 blocks to Fulton.

ARCHBISHOPS MANSION
Innkeepers: Jonathan Shannon & Jeffrey Ross
1000 Fulton Street
San Francisco, CA 94117
Tel: (415) 563-7872
15 bedrooms with private bathrooms
Double from $100 to $155
Open: all year
Credit cards: all major
Children accepted

It is a joy to visit the Inn at the Opera and see how with imagination, excellent taste and (of course) money, a mediocre hotel can be converted into a real gem. Stepping into the intimate lobby is like walking into a lovely home. Comfortable chairs slipcovered in muted green, a superb carpet with a rose design, an antique cabinet, potted palms, soft lighting and beautiful floral bouquets add to the mood of quiet elegance. From the reception area a hallway leads to one of San Francisco's most appealing small restaurants and cocktail lounge. Here, in the Act IV lounge, the ambiance changes from light and airy to cozy and romantic. Dark paisley-like print wallpaper, rich panelling, subdued lighting, leather upholstered chairs, green plants, beautiful flower arrangements, a baby grand piano softly playing and the open fireplace create the perfect rendezvous. The guest rooms maintain the same tasteful decor promised by the public rooms. Most have traditional furnishings in dark woods which contrast pleasantly with pastel walls, carpeting and drapes. The least expensive rooms are quite small, but even these have terrycloth robes in the armoire, small refrigerators, microwave ovens, direct-dial telephones and chocolates on the pillow. *Directions:* As you might guess from the name, the Inn at the Opera is located in the heart of San Francisco's Performing Arts Complex - a perfect hotel choice for patrons of the opera, ballet and symphony.

INN AT THE OPERA
Innkeeper: Annabella Wisniewski
333 Fulton Avenue
San Francisco, CA 94102
Tel: (415) 863-8400
48 bedrooms with private bathrooms
Double from $99 to $180
Open: all year
Credit cards: all major
Children accepted

The Inn at Union Square has an absolutely perfect location, smack in the heart of San Francisco - just steps from Union Square, the theaters and shopping. But it is not just its strategic position that makes this inn so appealing: it is a winner in every respect. The charm is apparent from the moment you enter into the cozy, book-lined lobby which looks more like a small library in a country home than a lobby in a commercial hotel. An elevator takes guests to the upper floors. As you step off the elevator, each floor has its own little sitting area where chairs are grouped comfortably around a fireplace and where complimentary tea is served each afternoon from 4:00PM to 6:00PM with sandwiches and cakes, followed in the early evening from 6:00PM to 8:00PM by wine and cheeses. Newspapers are left outside each door in the morning. Guests can either go to the lounge (the same one where tea and wine are served) for Continental breakfast or else they can have a tray brought to their room. The decor in each of the rooms is most attractive, with a traditional mood created by the use of beautiful fabrics and fine furniture. Some of the rooms have their own fireplaces and the penthouse suite has a jacuzzi tub. Every room, from the least expensive small room to the deluxe suites, is spotlessly maintained and very appealing. *Directions:* From Union Square take Post Street one block to the Inn at Union Square.

THE INN AT UNION SQUARE
Innkeeper: Brooks Bayly
400 Post Street
San Francisco, CA 94102
Tel: (415) 397-3510
30 bedrooms with private bathrooms
Double from $105 to $170
Open: all year
Credit cards: all major
Children accepted

The Marina Inn is not a typical country inn. In fact, it is a large, four-story building whose boxy exterior is made more lively by tiers of bay windows. But as soon as you enter, the successful effort to achieve the warmth of a homey inn is immediately apparent. The lobby is small and intimate, with light pine furniture, a pair of handsome upholstered chairs, green potted plants and off-white walls. The staff is friendly and eager to be helpful. An elevator leads upstairs to the bedrooms, each similar in decor with two-poster country beds, pastel print wallpaper, comfortable chairs, light pine armoires and forest green carpeting. In addition to being pleasantly decorated, the rooms offer all the amenities of a proper hotel: television in each room, comfortable queen-sized beds, direct-dial telephones and modern bathrooms with marble sinks and a basket of toiletries. On the second floor a sitting room is provided where in the morning a buffet Continental breakfast is served and in the afternoon complimentary sherry. One of the nicest merits of this hotel is its excellent price - a real value for such a spiffy place. Another plus: cribs are provided for babies and children under five are free of charge. The hotel is located just a brisk walk from Fisherman's Wharf, Ghirardelli Square and the Sir Francis Yacht Club. *Directions:* Take Van Ness Avenue north to Lombard Street. Turn left and go 3 blocks to Octavia.

MARINA INN
Innkeeper: Suzie Baum
3110 Octavia
San Francisco, CA 94123
Tel: (415) 928-1000
40 bedrooms with private bathrooms
Double from $55 to $85
Open: all year
Credit cards: all major
Children accepted

The Petite Auberge and the White Swan are two lovely little hotels sitting side by side on Bush Street in the heart of San Francisco. Both are owned and managed by the extremely clever "Four Sisters", a prestigious tiny chain of delightful little hotels in northern California. Whereas the White Swan has an English flavor, the Petite Auberge is like a romantic French country inn snuggled in the heart of San Francisco, just steps from the famous theater district and exclusive shopping and fine dining. The facade is most appealing - a narrow four-story building with a double column of bay windows bordered by narrow windows decorated with flower boxes. An antique carousel horse, burnished woods and soft pastel colors of peach and blue give a warm welcome to the cozy entry. Each guest room is attractively decorated with delicate colors. All have private baths, many have fireplaces, and each evening the linens are turned down and a flower and chocolates placed on the pillow. Wine and tea are served every afternoon to those guests who want a quiet moment after a busy day. A delicious breakfast is served buffet style each morning and includes a selection of teas and coffee, homemade breads, fruit, cereals and pastries. *Directions:* Take Van Ness Avenue north to Bush Street. Turn right on Bush and go approximately 1 mile. The inn is between Taylor and Mason.

PETITE AUBERGE
Innkeeper: Carolyn Vaughan
863 Bush Street
San Francisco, CA 94108
Tel: (415) 928-6000
26 bedrooms with private bathrooms
Double from $105 to $155
Open: all year
Credit cards: all major
Children accepted

The Sherman House is an oasis of luxury and provides San Francisco with some of its most exceptional accommodation and personalized and attentive service. This French Italianate three-story mansion was built in 1876 for Leander Sherman, founder of the Sherman Clay Music Company and host to a number of famous musicians who performed within its walls. A soaring, three-story music hall is now a stunning salon for hotel guests. The main house contains eleven rooms or suites, while the carriage house, set in the middle of the gardens designed by Thomas Church, offers three spectacular suites. Armoires, mirrors, desks, chairs, paintings and chandeliers have been carefully selected for each room. Each room has a grand canopy bed, sumptuously draped in luxurious fabrics with feather-down mattresses and a magnificent private bath finished in black granite with the exception of one in Chinese slate. The restaurant is open only to hotel residents and is spectacular when compared to any of the world's finest restaurants. The chef shops every day to obtain only the freshest and finest ingredients and plans his menu accordingly. *Directions:* From the south, take highway 101 to Franklin Street, bear left up the hill and continue for 18 blocks to Green Street. Turn left onto Green and continue 5 1/2 blocks to the Sherman House.

THE SHERMAN HOUSE
Innkeeper: Manou Mobedshahi
2160 Green Street
San Francisco, CA 94123
Tel: (415) 563-3600
14 bedrooms with private bathrooms
Double from $190 to $650
Open: all year
Credit cards: all major
Children accepted

The Spencer House does not look like a hotel and there is no sign in front of the beautiful old Victorian to give any clue that guests are welcome. Yet within this stately, immaculately maintained mansion is one of San Francisco's most personalized, delightful places to stay. The owners, Barbara and Jack Chambers, have converted a woefully neglected charmer back to its original glory - the attention to detail and the amount of love, labor and money that must have gone into the project is astounding: the floors gleam again as when first installed, Lincresta Walton wall coverings have been restored to their original perfection, the living room and bedrooms have been padded and "papered" with beautiful fabric to soften any distracting noises, the kitchen looks straight out of *Gourmet*, the original gas lights are still operable. Barbara took advantage of Jack being a commercial airline pilot and flew to London to pick out all of the exquisite fabrics and many of the gorgeous antiques used throughout. It is like being in a private home with each guest room exuding its own personality, but all, even the smallest, are most inviting. One of the greatest assets of the inn is Barbara, a superb hostess and a fabulous cook. Breakfast is always a memorable, gourmet event and dramatically presented using the finest china and silver. *Directions:* From Van Ness take Sutter Street to Divisidero, turn left to Haight then right for two blocks.

SPENCER HOUSE
Innkeepers: Barbara & Jack Chambers
1080 Haight Street
San Francisco, CA 94117
Tel: (415) 626-9205
6 Bedrooms with private bathrooms
Double from $75 to $150
Open: all year
Credit cards: none accepted
Children accepted over 16

The Washington Square Inn, one of San Francisco's most appealing hostelries, is located in the North Beach area, facing historic Washington Square. Within easy strolling distance is a wealth of wonderful little places to eat and a bit farther, but an interesting walk through Chinatown, are the theaters and shops of the Union Square area. From the moment you enter, the ambiance of the French countryside surrounds you - an antique dining table, mellowed with age and surrounded by country chairs, stretches in front of large windows framed with tie-back drapes. A superb armoire, large gilt mirror, baskets of flowers and a fireplace with an antique wooden mantel add to the country appeal. In the afternoon guests have tea in front of the fire and in the morning Continental breakfast is served here (if guests prefer, breakfast will be brought to their room). Two separate staircases lead to the guest rooms, each individually decorated with fine English and French antiques by the famous San Francisco designer Nan Rosenblatt (who, with her husband Norm, owns the inn). From the simplest room with "bath down the hall" to the most luxurious suite, each of the rooms exudes a lovely, elegant country charm. Beautiful coordinating fabrics dramatize the rooms, many with cozy bay windows accented with inviting sitting nooks. Each of the rooms has its own telephone. *Directions:* Located on Washington Square.

WASHINGTON SQUARE INN
Innkeeper: Brooks Bayley
1660 Stockton Street
San Francisco, CA 94133
Tel: (415) 981-4220
15 bedrooms, 10 with private bathrooms
Double from $65 to $160
Open: all year
Credit cards: all major
Children accepted

The White Swan Inn, a small, London-style hotel, has a spendid location just steps from a wide selection of quaint restaurants and a five-minute walk from San Francisco's fabulous Union Square shopping and theater district. Or, if you are heading for Fisherman's Wharf, the cable car is close by. But the appeal of the White Swan is far greater than its setting: from the moment you enter, you will know immediately that this is not a standard commercial hotel. A small sitting area greets you as you enter, with a reception desk to your right, but the heart of the inn is down a flight of stairs where a spacious lounge awaits with one section set up with tables and chairs for breakfast - a hearty meal of coffee, muffins, a hot entree, juices and cereals. Beyond the eating area is a pretty living room with a fireplace and comfortable lounge chairs. Next door is the library, another cozy area for relaxing. Although the inn is in the center of the city, French doors open out onto a small English-style garden where guests can sit outside on pleasant days. The bedrooms are beautifully decorated with pretty coordinating fabrics. Each room has a separate sitting area, fireplace (which can be turned on by a bedside switch), small refrigerator, wet bar, direct dial telephone and color television. *Directions:* Take Van Ness Avenue north to Bush Street. Turn right on Bush and go approximately 1 mile. The inn is between Taylor and Mason.

WHITE SWAN INN
Innkeeper: Carolyn Vaughan
845 Bush Street
San Francisco, CA 94108
Tel: (415) 775-1755
26 bedrooms with private bathrooms
Double from $145 to $160
Open: all year
Credit cards: all major
Children accepted

The Cheshire Cat is incorporated into two lovely beige and white Victorians sitting side by side near the center of Santa Barbara and connected by a tranquil bricked patio (where breakfast is served on all but grim days). Behind the patio a jacuzzi is sheltered by a lacy white gazebo. In the foyer a grouping of "Alice in Wonderland" figurines placed on a small table beside the guest book immediately sets the whimsical theme of the inn: each of the rooms is named for an Alice in Wonderland character with the exception of two rooms - Jean's (named for the owner Chris's mother) and the Eberle Suite (named for the previous owners). Laura Ashley coordinated prints and wallpapers are used throughout with different color schemes, from plums and creams in the Mad Hatter room to smoke-blue and cream in the Dormouse's Room. Each bedroom is different; some are dramatic with a large jacuzzi bath in the bedroom, some have cozy bay windows, others an intimate private balcony. Loving touches make each guest feel special: fresh flowers in the rooms, individual bottles of Baileys Cream, and delicious chocolates. The Cheshire Cat room has the added features of TV and VCR. Mountain bikes are available for guests with suggestions on where to pedal when exploring Santa Barbara. *Directions:* From highway 101 exit Arrallaga, proceed 4 blocks to Chapala and turn left for one block to Valerio.

THE CHESHIRE CAT
Innkeeper: Christine Dunstan
36 West Valerio Street
Santa Barbara, CA 93101
Tel: (805) 569-1610
11 bedrooms with private bathrooms
Double from $109 to $159
Open: all year
Credit cards: none accepted
Inappropriate for children

The El Encanto Hotel has the rare privilege of being the only hotel in an exclusive residential area in the foothills above Santa Barbara. As you drive into the parklike grounds, a central building houses the reception area and an intimate salon warmed by a cozy fireplace. With spectacular ocean views, a spacious bar decorated with dark wicker furniture overlooks two tiers of terraces banked with salmon pink geraniums which beautifully complement the pinks and greens of the interior decor. All the accommodations are in individual villas dotted spaciously about the lovely grounds. The decor varies greatly - some villas appear a bit drab while others which have been refurbished reflect great charm (if you like the old-world look, ask for one of the villas with country French decor). The styles of the buildings reflect various stages of development: those built in the '30s featuring heavy tiled roofs and dark wood-framed windows are definitely the most appealing. The villas are linked by a brick path which winds through the lovely gardens with fountains, a swimming pool, wisteria-covered arbors and reflecting pools - in summer the fragrance of jasmine scents the balmy air. *Directions:* Take Mission Road to the Mission Santa Barbara and, where the road forks, continue to the right a short distance to find Lasuen Road and the hotel on the left.

EL ENCANTO HOTEL
Innkeeper: Tom Narozonick
1900 Lasuen Road
Santa Barbara, CA 93103
Tel: (805) 687-5000 or (800) 346-7039
85 bedrooms with private bathrooms
Double from $100 to $300
Breakfast not included
Open: all year
Credit cards: all major
Children accepted

The Simpson House Inn, a handsome, rosy-beige Victorian with white and smoke blue trim, is superbly located on a quiet residential street only two blocks from the main shopping attractions of State Street. Surrounded by an acre of lawn, the back garden is especially appealing, with beautifully maintained flower beds and mature shade trees. One of the most irresistible features of the inn is a cheerful back porch under an arbor of draping wisteria with white wicker chairs and comfy pillows: a perfect niche to enjoy the garden. The lounges and dining room are quite formal - some museum-quality chairs are roped to prevent guests using them. However, the formality disappears upstairs in the charming guest chambers, each individually decorated to suit different tastes - some are lacy and frilly, others have a more tailored look. All are most attractive and enjoy such niceties as terry-cloth robes, fresh flowers, bottled water and decanters of Bristol Cream. The Simpson House has become so popular as an inn that the family has moved to another home to accommodate more guests though their touch is felt everywhere as they personally decorated every room. And, although their children are now off to college, their growth chart is still on the door of the cute telephone booth off the front hall. *Directions:* From downtown take Santa Barbara Street heading northeast toward the mission and turn left onto Arrellaga.

SIMPSON HOUSE INN
Innkeepers: Gillean Wilson & Linda Davies
121 East Arrellaga Street
Santa Barbara, CA 93101
Tel: (805) 963-7067
6 bedrooms, 5 with private bathrooms
Double from $85 to $130
Open: all year
Credit cards: MC, VS
Children accepted over 12

The Tiffany Inn is an especially handsome old Victorian separated by a lawn from a rather busy street in Santa Barbara's residential area. Although the traffic in front is a bit distracting, the back garden is very charming and gives a quiet retreat for guests with an attractive lattice-covered verandah set with prettily-covered wicker chairs. If you are a fan of beautifully decorated Victorians, you will thoroughly enjoy a stay at the Tiffany Inn. Carol has done a lovely job of decorating, with romantic, old-fashioned antiques accented by well-chosen, colorful fabrics. The living room with its grouping of sofas and chairs around a fireplace is just the perfect place to sit and relax while planning sightseeing adventures. Each comfortable bedchamber exudes its own charm and character and several have the added bonus of a cozy log-burning fireplace. For those who crave privacy, one of the rooms has its own outside entrance and the added bonus of breakfast delivered each morning on a tray. Other guests enjoy a hearty breakfast of fresh fruits, muffins and coffee served in the dining room or on sunny days in the peace and quiet of the lattice-covered porch in the back garden. Joining you for breakfast might be Tiffany, the perky black spaniel with a "diamond" collar. *Directions:* Exit highway 101 in Santa Barbara at Mission Street, drive east to De La Vina, turn left and the inn is on your right.

TIFFANY INN
Innkeepers: Carol & Larry MacDonald
1323 De la Vina Street
Santa Barbara, CA 93101
Tel: (805) 963-2283
6 bedrooms, 4 with private bathrooms
Double from $75 to $145
Open: all year
Credit cards: all major
Children accepted over 12

The Villa Rosa is beautifully located in Santa Barbara, only one half block from the beach. Whereas most of our recommendations in this town reflect the Victorian era, the Villa Rosa has a Spanish style - built of adobe with liberal use of arches, wrought iron balconies, heavy wooden beams and an authentic red-tiled roof. The small hotel fronts right onto the street but inside is an oasis of quiet. You enter into a lovely terra-cotta tiled hallway and a staircase leading up to the bedrooms. The lobby is right off the entry with a small reception desk and a fireplace which blazes in winter offering a cheery reception. Large French doors open out to a delightful, secluded patio with a swimming pool surrounded by flowers. Light wooden shutters, simple wooden furnishings, wicker baskets filled with greenery and terra-cotta planters give a simple, Santa Fe-Mexican look, while muted earth-toned fabrics lend a masculine air - especially to the guest rooms. There is a wide selection of rooms - from a simple bedroom to a large suite equipped with its own kitchenette - some rooms have fireplaces. The Villa Rosa exudes the warmth of a bed and breakfast with the professionalism and services of a sophisticated hotel - combining such niceties as 24-hour service and the Los Angeles Times at your door each morning with chocolates and roses on your pillow at night. *Directions:* Take 101 south to Chapala Street and turn right.

THE VILLA ROSA
Innkeeper: Beverly Kirkhart
15 Chapala Street
Santa Barbara, CA 93101
Tel: (805) 966-0851
18 bedrooms with private bathrooms
Double from $90 to $185
Open: all year
Credit cards: all major
Children accepted over 14

The 550-acre San Ysidro Ranch is nestled in the foothills of the Santa Ynez mountains. It has a wonderful history of hospitality dating back to the 1890s when the ranch was used as a way station for Franciscan monks: later, famous writers such as Sinclair Lewis and Somerset Maughan came here to write. During the period the ranch was owned by the movie star Ronald Colman, it became a hideaway for the rich and famous - Vivien Leigh and Laurence Olivier were married at the ranch and Jackie and John F. Kennedy honeymooned here. Today the ranch is run as an exclusive small resort, still attracting guests who want to escape the hubbub of city life to relax in a rustic setting yet be properly pampered. All of the accommodations are in separate cottages which vary in appearance; most are like modern ranch-style homes carefully positioned to provide privacy. The decor in those that have been refurbished in a country motif with brass beds and comfy quilts are more attractive than some of the others. Although many guests never leave their own "home", the resort offers a lovely swimming pool, tennis courts and horseback riding. There is an excellent restaurant on the property - guests can come to dine here or order room service. *Directions:* From highway 101 take the San Ysidro exit east toward the mountains. After passing East Valley Road take the San Ysidro Lane to the right, weaving up to the hotel.

SAN YSIDRO RANCH
Innkeeper: Jan Martin Winn
900 San Ysidro Lane
Montecito, CA 93108
Tel: (805) 969-5046
43 bedrooms with private bathrooms
Double from $160 to $285
Open: all year
Credit cards: all major
Children accepted

The foundations of The Babbling Brook Inn date back to the 1790s when padres from the Santa Cruz mission built a grist mill on the property, taking advantage of the small stream to grind corn. At the end of the 19th century a tannery powered by a huge water wheel was constructed. Then, a few years later, a rustic log cabin was built and remains today as the "heart" of the inn with a small lobby where guests congregate about a roaring fire with hot coffee and homemade cookies. Most of the guest rooms are in shingled chalets nestled in the garden surrounded by pines and redwoods and overlooking the idyllic little meandering brook. Each of the rooms is decorated in European country style with an individual flair. Although calling itself a "bed and breakfast", The Babbling Brook is actually wonderfully sophisticated - each of the 12 guest rooms has a private bathroom, telephone, radio with alarm, and television. Most have a cozy fireplace, private deck and an outside entrance - two have deep, soaking, jet bathtubs. The owners, Tom and Helen King, add greatly to the warmth and charm of this appealing little inn. Tom, who was previously a commercial airline president, now is the gracious host. Helen, who has won many awards for her cooking, not only keeps guests well supplied with cookies, but also serves a delicious full breakfast each morning. *Directions:* From Pacific Coast highway 1 take Laurel Street two blocks west toward the Ocean.

THE BABBLING BROOK INN
Innkeepers: Tom & Helen King
1025 Laurel Street
Santa Cruz, CA 95060
Tel: (408) 427-2437
12 bedrooms with private bathrooms
Double from $85 to $125
Open: all year
Credit cards: all major
Children accepted over 12

Sausalito is a quaint waterfront town with fabulous views across the bay to San Francisco. Alongside the harbor runs one main street from which small roads spider-web up the steep hillside checkered with many Victorian houses. Among these is a lovely home, built in 1885, with marble fireplaces, stained glass windows, wrought-iron grillework and lacy wood trim, which has now been converted to a wonderful hotel. The dining room and a few of the guest rooms are in the original home, while the rest of the rooms are in clusters of small buildings which step down the hill to the main street. The guest rooms in the original Victorian have been refurbished in Victorian style with all the behind-the-scenes amenities added for modern comfort. The newer rooms (many with views) are larger and each has its own style of decor - to mention just a few: Casa Cabana has a southwest look; Misia's Lilac and Lace is all fancy with eyelet and laces; La Belle Provence is very French, done in blues and whites; The Summer House is light and airy with light woods and wicker furniture; the Artist's Loft is most appealing with a fresh, uncluttered New-England look. The restaurant, with its large glassed-in porch, is a favorite, not only for guests of the hotel, but also for San Franciscans who come over for dinner or lunch. *Directions:* Ferry from San Francisco or 101 over the Golden Gate Bridge. Take the Alexander exit which becomes Bridgeway.

CASA MADRONA HOTEL
Innkeeper: John W. Mays
801 Bridgeway
Sausalito, CA 94965
Tel: (415) 332-0502
34 bedrooms with private bathrooms
Double from $80 to $175
Open: all year
Credit cards: all major
Children accepted

El Ranchito is secluded on an oak-studded hillside which shelters a beautiful little valley threading between the towns of Los Olivos and Solvang. The inn is reached off Alamo Pintado Road on a tiny private lane lined with roses and rosemary which winds up the hillside to a lovely, large Spanish home and two tiny casitas. The large house belongs to the owners, Don and Joan Speirs, while the two casitas on the property are for guests. The first casita, Villa Fiori, is reached by a flight of steps leading up from the parking area; the second is located near the main house but, facing a different view, has complete privacy. Both are most appealingly built of adobe with heavy tiled roofs. From their travels, Don and Joan have brought home treasures from Europe such as Italian sinks, French windows and antique accent pieces which have been incorporated into the rooms. Our favorite is Villa Amore, with a fireplace, blue-checked comfy sofa, country-cozy decor and a private patio with a view of the hills. Breakfast is a scrumptious meal with Danish pastries from neighboring Solvang, homemade sausage, eggs collected from the farm (when the hens cooperate), coffee, fruits and juice. *Directions:* From Solvang drive north on the 246 to Alamo Pintado Road. Turn left and continue 1.8 miles. Turn left at a tiny lane marked with a small sign reading "El Ranchito".

EL RANCHITO
Innkeeper: Joan Speirs
1451 Alamo Pintado Road
Solvang, CA 93463
Tel: (805) 688-9360
2 cottages with private bathrooms
Double $115
Open: all year
Credit cards: none accepted
Children accepted by special arrangement

Although a modern-day hotel, the Tivoli Inn, located in the heart of the Danish-style village of Solvang, strongly reflects the old-world European flavor of the town. A whimsical clock tower highlights the medieval-looking facade of the hotel whose roofline is an appealing jumble of gables. The front lobby is tiny - pleasantly uncommercial in appearance and with a staff to greet you that is most gracious. Although this is definitely a polished, sophisticated hotel, the ambiance is one of a country inn. The guest rooms are nestled on various levels, most with their own outdoor entrance, giving an individual cottage look to each. Chilled wine and a basket of fresh fruit are brought to each room soon after check-in and in the morning hot coffee, juice and marvelous Solvang pastries appear - homey touches for a larger hotel. The bedrooms (mostly suites) are extremely attractive with a comfy, country ambiance - color-coordinated wallpapers and fabrics are used throughout. All but two have freestanding fireplaces and wood is provided. Rather than having the standard hotel look, the bedrooms are designed with imagination - such as stepping up to a small eating nook or down to a cozy fireplace setting. For guests flying into Santa Barbara, limousine service to the hotel can be arranged. *Directions:* From highway 101 take highway 246 east toward Solvang. Turn right on 5th Street and left on Copenhagen Drive.

TIVOLI INN
Innkeeper: Les Clark
1564 Copenhagen Drive
Solvang, CA 93463
Tel: (805) 688-0559
29 bedrooms with private bathrooms
Double from $85 to $190
Open: all year
Credit cards: all major
Children accepted

The approach to the Trout Farm (through a suburban area of Solvang) is not outstanding, but once you drive down the lane leading to the inn, the modern mood changes dramatically and you will think you are in the Swedish countryside. Northwest of Stockholm there is an idyllic area called Dalarna where pretty old farmhouses, painted barn-house red with crisp white trim, dot the landscape - the Trout Farm looks like one of these. The 90-year-old farmhouse has two simply furnished bedrooms, both with a fireplace and a private bathroom. Between the two guest rooms is an unpretentious, cozy parlor where guests can sip hot chocolate in front of the fire. Outside a grassy lawn, dotted with shade trees, sweeps down to a pond which was used at one time as a fish hatchery (accounting for the inn's name). Just a few steps from the pond there is a small cottage where another bedroom and bath are located. With a total of only three bedrooms, you will never feel surrounded by civilization, so if you want a non-sophisticated, homey retreat with a quiet, rural simplicity, the Trout Farm might be perfect. The inn is owned by Don and Joan Speirs who also own El Ranchito, another tiny countryside inn near Solvang. *Directions:* Take highway 246 north from Solvang for approximately 2 miles and turn right on Carriage. Turn right again at the first road (Covered Wagon) which deadends at the Trout Farm.

TROUT FARM
Innkeeper: Sylvia Roofe
2844 Covered Wagon Road
Solvang, CA 93463
Tel: (805) 688-9517
3 bedrooms with private bathrooms
Double $95
Open: all year
Credit cards: none accepted
Children accepted

Overview Farm is one of Sonoma's most romantic getaways and, with only three rooms, Judy and Robert Weiss provide personalized service for each of their guests. Secluded on 5 acres, the home, built as part of the Spreckles' family estate, is a single-story, white shingle house with porches on two sides. Hardwood floors in the public areas, 12-foot ceilings and paned windows looking out to vineyard views provide the basis of the decor. The living room and dining rooms are both casually elegant and the bedrooms, named for local wine districts, are beautifully furnished, luxuriously appointed and individual in their appeal. The Alexander Valley room has a magnificent cannonball bed, a country hutch with a handsome display of pewter, a flaxen wheel, walls hung with samplers and a separate, cozy sitting room. The Dry Creek room has a dramatic, lace-covered canopy bed and quilted armchairs before a lovely brick fireplace enframed by a handsome wood mantel. The Carneros room is Victorian in decor, enjoys a wonderful fireplace and an enormous marble bathroom. All the rooms are lovely - and, rather than choose between them, a minimum of three visits is recommended. *Directions:* From Sonoma travel north on highway 12 for 4 miles, take a left on Madrone, follow Madrone to its end and then take a left on Arnold Drive. Go about 300 yards to a white post with four white arrows, turn right and continue uphill through pillars.

OVERVIEW FARM
Innkeepers: Judy & Robert Weiss
15650 Arnold Drive
Sonoma, CA 95476
Tel: (707) 938-8574
3 bedrooms with private bathrooms
Double $92.50
Open: all year
Credit cards: none accepted
Inappropriate for children

The town of Sonoma is a gem and a wonderful base for exploring the region, its wineries and points of historical interest. Because of the part it played in California's history it is a fascinating destination for children, and the Sonoma Hotel, located on a corner of the main plaza, is one of the few hotels in the area that welcomes them. The Sonoma Hotel is also a historical landmark, housed in a century-old building which has offered overnight accommodation for decades. You can enter the hotel through its attractive lobby or into a delightful old-fashioned saloon. Casual dining is possible in the restaurant set with antique oak tables or, when weather permits, on the shaded garden patio. A steep flight of stairs leads to the upstairs bedrooms. Hallways are papered to capture a feeling of yesteryear and decorated with lovely antiques, mementos and plants. All of the seventeen bedrooms have been thoughtfully furnished with antiques to enhance both the flavor and history of the hotel. The five rooms with private bath have deep, clawfoot tubs. In the European tradition, all other rooms have private washbasins and share bathrooms on the hallways. The inn's owners oversee every aspect of innkeeping. *Directions:* From San Francisco take highway 101 north: go travel east on highway 37 to highway 121 and then north on highway 12 to the northwest corner of Sonoma's plaza.

SONOMA HOTEL
Innkeeper: Sue Marino
110 West Spain Street
Sonoma, CA 95476
Tel: (707) 996-2996
17 bedrooms, 5 with private bathrooms
Double from $58 to $98
Open: all year
Credit cards: all major
Children accepted

Sutter Creek is a charming gold country town whose main street is bordered at either end by New-England style residences surrounded by green lawns and neatly clipped hedges. Occupying one of these attractive homes is The Foxes, an idyllic hideaway put together with great flair and taste by Pete and Min Fox. The symbol of the inn is the fox and the perky little fellow pops up everywhere. Yet this is not an inn with a cutesy theme, but an unsnobbish, sophisticated inn where everything has been done with exquisite flair. Three suites are in the main house and three new suites have been added to the rear. The Honeymoon Suite is the largest, most elegant bedchamber where a large brick fireplace overlooks a magnificent bed, gorgeous Austrian armoire and very old English blanket chest. Sparkling crystal chandeliers light the enormous bathroom. In the Foxes' Den a border of foxes, hunt prints, a hunting horn, leatherbound books and leather chairs set before the fireplace give the room an inviting study feel. Each suite has a sitting area with a table to accommodate breakfast. Pete and Min discuss with you what you would like for breakfast and then it is brought to your room on silver service accompanied by a large pot of coffee or tea. You feel thoroughly pampered by a stay here. *Directions:* Sutter Creek straddles highway 49, 4 miles north of Jackson. The Foxes is on your left at the end of Main Street.

THE FOXES
Innkeepers: Pete & Min Fox
77 Main Street
Sutter Creek, CA 95685
Tel: (209) 267-5882
6 suites with private bathrooms
Double from $80 to $120
Open: all year
Credit cards: MC, VS
Inappropriate for children

Both of our featured Sutter Creek inns have their own motif. Where The Foxes has foxes The Hanford House has bears, a living room full of bears, whimsical characters smiling down from high shelves or peeking shyly over the back of the sofa, and 5-foot tall Freddie at his post: lounging in his chair at the front door to welcome guests. The "guest register" is a bit unusual - not a book at all, but rather the adjacent breakfast room walls and ceiling: upon departure each guest is handed a special marking pen and adds his name and perhaps a funny note or cartoon. It seems a bit strange, but actually comes off very well, making a most original "wallpaper". Jim and Lucille cleverly pull it all together and are as fun-loving as the atmosphere they have created. (I must admit that the whole theme made a very refreshing change from the hundreds of versions of country cute that I looked at.) The bedrooms are attractive, with delightfully uncluttered, plain white walls, coordinated drapes and bedspreads, pine armoires and headboards - and, of course, a teddy or two. *Directions:* Sutter Creek straddles highway 49, 4 miles north of Jackson. At the end of Main street follow the 49 round to the left and The Hanford House is immediately on your left.

THE HANFORD HOUSE
Innkeepers: Jim & Lucille Jacobus
61 Hanford Street, P.O. Box 1450
Sutter Creek, CA 95685
Tel: (209) 267-0747
8 bedrooms with private bathrooms
Double from $55 to $100
Open: all year
Credit cards: MC, VS
Children accepted over 15

My idea of a holiday at Lake Tahoe is to rent a cabin in the pines and catch up on my reading. One can do just that at The Cottage Inn which captures the mountain-cabin atmosphere while adding the comforts of fresh linens and a scrumptious breakfast. Built as a resort by the Pomin family in 1938, the cottages (which recently received a major overhaul without sacrificing their knotty pine panelling) are grouped under the pines a few steps from the shore of the lake. In the guest rooms Swedish-pine furniture and a variety of beds (brass, willow or pine) are complemented by the use of rich colors. The Fireplace Room has the added attraction of a wood-burning fireplace. The Pomin House, the original home on the property, contains the reception area, a large sitting room with games, books and comfortable furniture before a blazing log fire, and the breakfast room. In summer you can happily while away the hours sunning yourself on the dock and swimming in Lake Tahoe's cool, clear waters; the more energetic can take advantage of the lovely bicycle trail that passes behind the inn. Vikingsholm, Emerald Bay and D. L. Bliss Park are a short car-ride south. Ski resorts are between a 5-minute and 20-minute drive distant. *Directions:* From the Bay Area take the I 80 to the 89 Tahoe City exit, follow the river to Tahoe City and continue south on the 89 following West Lake Boulevard: the inn is 2 miles on your left.

THE COTTAGE INN
Innkeepers: Phil & Carol Brubaker
1690 West Lake Blvd, P.O. Box 66
Tahoe City, CA 95730
Tel: (916) 581-4073
15 bedrooms with private bathrooms
Double from $90 to $125
Open: all year
Credit cards: MC, VS
Children under 12 accepted in family suite

Having just visited a nearby inn where we were made to feel thoroughly unwelcome, it was with some trepidation that we knocked on the door of Mayfield House. But after a most gracious greeting from Stephanie, our mood once again was "up". The experience was a good one - emphasizing so personally the great importance of an innkeeper's warmth of reception. Mayfield House is a cozy wood and stone building just a short walk from Lake Tahoe and the center of Tahoe City. The living room with its dark pine panelling, beamed ceiling, large fireplace and sofas is very comfortable and inviting. There are only six bedrooms sharing the facilities of three bathrooms (bathrobes are provided). Bedrooms are priced according to the size of the room and the bed. The innkeepers do not live at the inn so if you arrive late in the day you will be left a key and a friendly welcoming note explaining how things work. A breakfast of fresh fruit, muffins and a hot beverage is served in the breakfast room or on the patio. Guests are encouraged to make themselves hot beverages in the tiny kitchen. A shed on the patio is used for storing ski equipment - Squaw Valley and several other ski resorts are just a ten-minute drive away. *Directions:* From the Bay Area take the I 80 to the 89 Tahoe City exit and follow the river to Tahoe City: Grove Street is on your left.

MAYFIELD HOUSE
Innkeepers: Stephanie Smith & Janie Kaye
236 Grove Street, P.O. Box 5999
Tahoe City, CA 95730
Tel: (916) 583-1001
6 bedrooms sharing 3 bathrooms
Double from $65 to $100
Open: all year
Credit cards: MC, VS
Children accepted over 10

Lake Tahoe is an exquisite, crystal-clear blue lake ringed by pines and backed by high mountains. The only outlet for this enormous body of water is the Truckee River, and standing on a broad river bend some 3 miles downstream is River Ranch. This lodge exudes the air of a mountain resort, and the circular bar with its picture windows opening onto the river is particularly popular with the winter apres-ski crowd. The bedrooms are most attractively decorated in soft pastels with matching drapes and bedspreads in country check fabrics - all the rooms have phones, televisions and river views. The very nicest have queen-size beds and private balconies, while one very inexpensive tiny room has bunk beds. The ski resorts of Squaw Valley, Deer Park and Alpine Meadows are all close at hand for winter fun, with sightseeing, hiking, trout fishing and river rafting as favorite summer pastimes. If you are not inclined to physical disportment, you can confine yourself to the patio and watch rafters hurtle down the last stretch of their river ride and scramble ashore. Rafting the gentle Truckee river is a fun family outing. A basic Continental breakfast of sweet rolls, muffins and beverages is served in the bar. *Directions:* From the Bay Area take the I 80 to the 89 Tahoe City exit and follow the river to River Ranch.

RIVER RANCH
Innkeeper: Marlene Block
P.O. Box 197
2285 River Ranch Road
Tahoe City, CA 95730
Tel: (916) 583-4264
23 bedrooms with private bathrooms
Double from $50 to $75
Open: all year
Credit cards: all major
Children accepted

The Country House Inn is located on the main street of Templeton, a pretty, small, western-style town, about midway between Los Angeles and San Francisco. The building, a large, white Victorian farmhouse accented by a dusty rose trim, is surrounded by a wide, grassy lawn dotted with shade trees and set off by an old-fashioned white picket fence. The inn is simple, not decorated with the polish of an expensive interior designer, yet abounding with the warmth and good taste of the owner, Dianne Garth, who bought the property a few years ago and has been pouring love and money into it ever since. Roses climbing over the porch set the mood as you enter the comfortable house. The dining room, a bright and airy room with flower-sprigged wallpaper and French doors leading to the garden, is the heart of the inn, with light wooden chairs and an antique country table. Country accents abound, especially a wonderful collection of hobbyhorses. Many of the very attractive handmade items are for sale. Each of the guest rooms is individually decorated and has its own personality. The front parlor room is decorated in shades of pink with Laura Ashley fabrics. The porch room, decorated in happy yellows, has its own private entrance. *Directions:* Twenty miles north of San Luis Obispo on highway 101, turn off 101 at Vineyard, turn right to Second Street, then turn left after about 1 mile onto Main Street.

COUNTRY HOUSE INN
Innkeeper: Dianne Garth
91 Main Street
Templeton, CA 93465
Tel: (805) 434-1598
5 bedrooms, 1 with private bathroom
Double from $65 to $80
Open: all year
Credit cards: MC, VS
Children accepted

The Trinidad Bed & Breakfast is a Cape Cod-style home contructed in 1949, painted barn-red with crisp white trim, located just across the road from the Trinidad Lighthouse. Although neither the building nor the furnishings are old, this small inn is very inviting. You enter into a light and airy family room with a brick fireplace faced by a sofa and flanked by two wooden rockers. Against the wall a small area is set up to display a selection of handmade gift items that are offered for sale. In the kitchen a table is set prettily for the breakfast which consists of homemade jams and hot baked bread or muffins. Downstairs there is a simple twin-bedded room while upstairs are two more double rooms, each with an alcove in the dormer with views of the coast. Above the garage is the fourth bedroom with the best view of all from its long strip of windows overlooking the harbor. There is nothing outstanding in the decor, but then there is no pretence: this is just a homelike inn, but immaculately clean with everything shining with a "just scrubbed" look. The best part of all is the location: overlooking Trinidad Bay, whose old wharf still looks like a proper wharf should and where the trails along the magnificent headlands still maintain their unspoilt splendor. *Directions:* 25 miles north of Eureka on highway 101. Take the Trinidad exit west to Trinidad Bay Lighthouse - the inn is across the street.

TRINIDAD BED & BREAKFAST
Innkeepers: Carol & Paul Kirk
560 Edwards Street
Trinidad, CA 95570
Tel: (707) 677-0840
4 bedrooms with private bathrooms
Double from $65 to $95
Open: all year
Credit cards: none accepted
Children accepted over 10

The Carrville Inn, located in the Trinity Alps, began its history as a wayside inn for stagecoaches on their way to Oregon. The inn has great architectural appeal, a simple, white, wooden building with a two-tiered porch stretching across the front where guests sit in old-fashioned wicker furniture to soak in the view of the meadow and hills. A shady lawn with a lazy swing hung from the tree, a swimming pool enclosed by a white picket fence, and Crystal, the pet horse, munching apples from the tree complete the scene of tranquility. Downstairs the mood is "light" Victorian. The furnishings are appropriate to the era, but are not dark and oppressive - especially in the dining room, the mood is bright, with large windows overlooking the rose garden. Upstairs there are five bedrooms, three with private bathrooms and two sharing a large bathroom. Each room is most attractively decorated and has its own personality. The inn is very professionally run and guests are pampered from the time they come down to Barbara's hearty country breakfast (featuring farm-fresh eggs) until they retire at night to bedlinens turned down, the lamps softly lit, a pitcher of icewater beside the bed and chocolates on the pillow. *Directions:* To reach the Carrville Inn, take highway 3 north from Weaverville and continue 6 miles past Trinity Center to the Carrville Loop Road (the first paved road you will come to on your left).

CARRVILLE INN
Innkeepers: Barbara & Ray Vasconcellos
Carrville Loop Road
Trinity Center, CA 96091
Tel: (916) 266-3511
5 bedrooms, 3 with private bathrooms
Double from $75 to $100
Open: all year
Credit cards: none accepted
Children accepted over 16

Tuolumne is a modest old mining and lumbering town on a delightful gold country backroad. On the town's outskirts, set high on a tree-shaded knoll surrounded by 56 acres of hills and valleys, is Oak Hill Ranch. Arriving at this graceful yellow and white Victorian home you feel you have stepped back into the last century; but the house was built in 1980. Sanford and Jane Grover collected Victoriana for over 25 years before they and their architect son designed a house to incorporate their treasures: a grand staircase, a stained glass window, door trims, fireplace mantels and porch railings. When their children and grandchildren moved nearby, Jane and Sanford no longer needed so much space, so they opened their home to guests. Indoors everything reflects the Victorian era - right down to Sanford and Jane who dress in Victorian costume, she in ruffled cap and long skirt, he in starched shirt and arm bands to serve guests a lavish breakfast at the dining room table. I much prefered the bedrooms in the main house to those in the rustic cottage. The Eastlake bedroom, furnished with classic Eastlake furniture with its simple lines and high wooden headboard is a particularly handsome room. *Directions:* From Sonora take highway 108 east to Tuolumne. Turn right on Carter Street, left on Elm for 1 block, right on Apple Colony Road for 1/2 mile and Oak Hill Ranch is signposted up a private road on your left.

OAK HILL RANCH
Innkeepers: Sanford & Jane Grover
18550 Connally Lane, P.O. Box 307
Tuolumne, CA 95379
Tel: (209) 928-4717
5 bedrooms, 3 with private bathrooms
Double from $60 to $85
Open: all year
Credit cards: none accepted
Children accepted over 15

Contra Costa County by and large comprises bedroom communities for San Francisco commuters. Walnut Creek is one of its more attractive towns, having the advantages of both freeways and the fast, high-tech BART trains (Bay Area Rapid Transit) to whisk you into San Francisco. Surprisingly, this urban enclave has a perfect hideaway inn for those who want to get away from San Francisco and yet cannot travel very far. The Mansion at Lakewood is a lovely Victorian estate sitting behind high, white, wrought-iron gates in a quiet residential neighborhood of ranch-style homes. Sharyn and Mike McCoy bought the then dilapidated home and wrangled with the city council to be able to restore it and open it as a country inn. Their battle won, The Mansion has received a new lease on life with luxurious appointments and inviting decor. The bedrooms range from the cozy Attic Hideaway to the opulent Estate Suite where an extraordinary antique four-poster brass bed draped with lace and soft pink damask sits center stage. The suite's enormous bathroom has every luxurious amenity: jacuzzi tub, extra large shower, his and hers vanities, oodles of soft towels and fluffy robes. A breakfast of hot, flaky, homemade croissants and fresh fruit is exquisitely presented. *Directions:* From highway 680 take Ygnacio Valley Road north, turn right on Homestead and left on Hacienda: downtown Walnut Creek is just 1/4 mile away.

THE MANSION AT LAKEWOOD
Innkeepers: Sharyn & Mike McCoy
1056 Hacienda Drive
Walnut Creek, CA 94598
Tel: (415) 946-9075
7 bedrooms with private bathrooms
Double from $95 to $195
Open: all year
Credit cards: MC, VS
Children accepted over 13

The Ahwahnee with 123 bedrooms hardly qualifies for inclusion in a country inn guide. It is a large, bustling resort with a level of activity in its lobby that is comparable to that at many airports, yet it merits inclusion because it is the most individual of hotels, with all the sophistication of a grand European castle, surrounded by the awesome beauty of Yosemite Valley. The lofty vastness of the lounge dwarfs the sofas and chairs and its huge windows frame magnificent views of the outdoors. The dining room has to be the largest in the United States: it is gorgeous with its massive floor-to-ceiling windows framing towering granite walls, cascading waterfalls and giant sugar pines. In contrast to the surrounding wilderness the dining room wears an air of sophistication in the evening when guests dress for dinner and flickering candlelight casts its magical spell. Bedrooms are in the main building or in little cottages in a nearby woodland grove. There is a small swimming pool just off the back patio and it is not unusual to see deer grazing on the lawn. This is undeniably a grand old hotel but if the pricetag is a little rich for your blood, less expensive accommodations in Yosemite Valley are briefly outlined on page 53. *Directions:* The Ahwahnee is located in Yosemite Valley just east of Yosemite Village.

THE AHWAHNEE
Innkeeper: Bill Wymore
Yosemite National Park, CA 95389
Tel: (209) 372-1407
Reservations: (209) 252-4848
123 bedrooms & cottages with private bathrooms
Double from $175 to $225
Breakfast not included
Open: all year
Credit cards: all major
Children accepted

While the attractions of staying in Yosemite Valley cannot be denied, a more serene, country atmosphere pervades the Wawona Hotel, located within Yosemite Park about a 27-mile drive south of the valley. With its shaded verandahs overlooking broad, rolling lawns and a nine-hole golf course, the hotel presents a welcoming picture that invites one to while away the afternoon beside the pool, fondly referred to as the swimming tank. Bedrooms are in several scattered buildings and private bathrooms are at a premium. Bedrooms without private facilities use two blocks of men's and women's bathrooms, which can be situated a long walk from your bedroom. The hotel was refurbished in 1987 in a most attractive decor. This is the kind of wonderful old hotel that attracts lots of families: people who came as children now return with their children and grandchildren. Advance dinner reservations are recommended. In the summer rangers give interpretive presentations on such topics as bears, climbing and photography and there are carriage rides, wonderful Sunday brunches, Saturday-night barbecues and barn dances. *Directions:* Wawona is in Yosemite National Park, 27 miles south of Yosemite Valley on highway 41.

WAWONA HOTEL
Innkeeper: Judy Durr
Yosemite National Park, CA 95389
Tel: (209) 375-6556
Reservations: (209) 252-4848
105 bedrooms, 52 with private bathrooms
Double from $55 to $70
Breakfast not included
Open: Mar 17th to Oct 30th, then weekends only
Open for Presidents' holidays, Christmas & New Year
Credit cards: all major
Children accepted

Map Section

PLACES TO STAY IN NORTHERN CALIFORNIA

24 Monterey, Old Monterey Inn, 165
25 Pacific Grove, Gosby House, 174
25 Pacific Grove, The Green Gables Inn, 175
25 Pacific Grove, The House of Seven Gables Inn, 176
26 Aptos, Mangels House, 105
27 Santa Cruz, The Babbling Brook Inn, 15, 206
28 Palo Alto, The Victorian on Lytton, 180
29 Moss Beach, Seal Cove Inn, 167
30 San Francisco, Archbishops Mansion, 191
30 San Francisco, Inn at the Opera, 192
30 San Francisco, The Inn at Union Square, 193
30 San Francisco, Marina Inn, 194
30 San Francisco, Petite Auberge, 195
30 San Francisco, The Sherman House, 196
30 San Francisco, Spencer House, 197
30 San Francisco, Washington Square Inn, 198
30 San Francisco, White Swan Inn, 199
31 Walnut Creek, The Mansion at Lakewood, 222
32 Point Richmond, East Brother Light Station, 182
33 Sausalito, Casa Madrona Hotel, 207
34 Muir Beach, Pelican Inn, 70, 168
35 Point Reyes Station, Thirty-nine Cypress, 181
36 Inverness, Blackthorne Inn, 146
36 Inverness, The Dancing Coyote Beach, 70, 147
36 Inverness, Ten Inverness Way, 148
37 Napa, La Residence, 170
37 Napa, Oakville Ranch, 171
38 Sonoma, Overview Farm, 211
38 Sonoma, Sonoma Hotel, 212
39 Glen Ellen, Beltane Ranch, 97, 136
40 St Helena, Ink House, 185
40 St Helena, Meadowood Resort Hotel, 91, 186
40 St Helena, Hotel St Helena, 187
40 St Helena, The Wine Country Inn, 188
41 Calistoga, The Elms Bed & Breakfast, 108
41 Calistoga, Foothill House, 109
41 Calistoga, Larkmead Country Inn, 110
41 Calistoga, Meadowlark Country House, 95, 111
41 Calistoga, Mount View Hotel, 112
42 Healdsburg, Belle de Jour Inn, 140
42 Healdsburg, Haydon House, 141
42 Healdsburg, Healdsburg Inn on the Plaza, 142
42 Healdsburg, Madrona Manor, 74, 143
43 Guerneville, The Estate, 139
44 Cloverdale, Ye Olde Shelford House, 123
45 Gualala, Old Milano Hotel, 138
46 Elk, Elk Cove Inn, 130
46 Elk, Harbor House, 131
47 Albion, Albion River Inn, 104
48 Little River, Glendeven, 155
48 Little River, Heritage House, 75, 156
49 Mendocino, Blue Heron Inn, 160
49 Mendocino, The Headlands Inn, 161
49 Mendocino, Joshua Grindle Inn, 162
49 Mendocino, Mendocino Farmhouse, 163
49 Mendocino, The Stanford Inn by the Sea, 164
50 Garberville, Benbow Inn, 134
51 Ferndale, The Gingerbread Mansion, 79, 133
52 Eureka, The Carter House Country Inn, 132
53 Trinidad, Trinidad Bed & Breakfast, 219
54 Trinity Center, Carrville Inn, 81, 220
55 McCloud, McCloud Guest House, 159
56 Quincy, The Feather Bed, 183
57 Nevada City, Grandmere's, 172
58 Grass Valley, Murphy's Inn, 61, 137
59 Tahoe, The Cottage Inn, 215
59 Tahoe, Mayfield House, 216
59 Tahoe, River Ranch, 63, 217
60 Georgetown, American River Inn, 135
61 Coloma, Coloma Country Inn, 125
62 Sutter Creek, The Foxes, 59, 213
62 Sutter Creek, The Hanford House, 60, 214
63 Murphys, Dunbar House, 1880, 169
64 Columbia, City Hotel, 55, 126
64 Columbia, Fallon Hotel, 55, 127
65 Jamestown, Jamestown Hotel, 55, 149
66 Tuolumne, Oak Hill Ranch, 221
67 Yosemite, The Ahwahnee, 53, 223
67 Yosemite, Wawona Hotel, 54, 224

Map I - Northern California

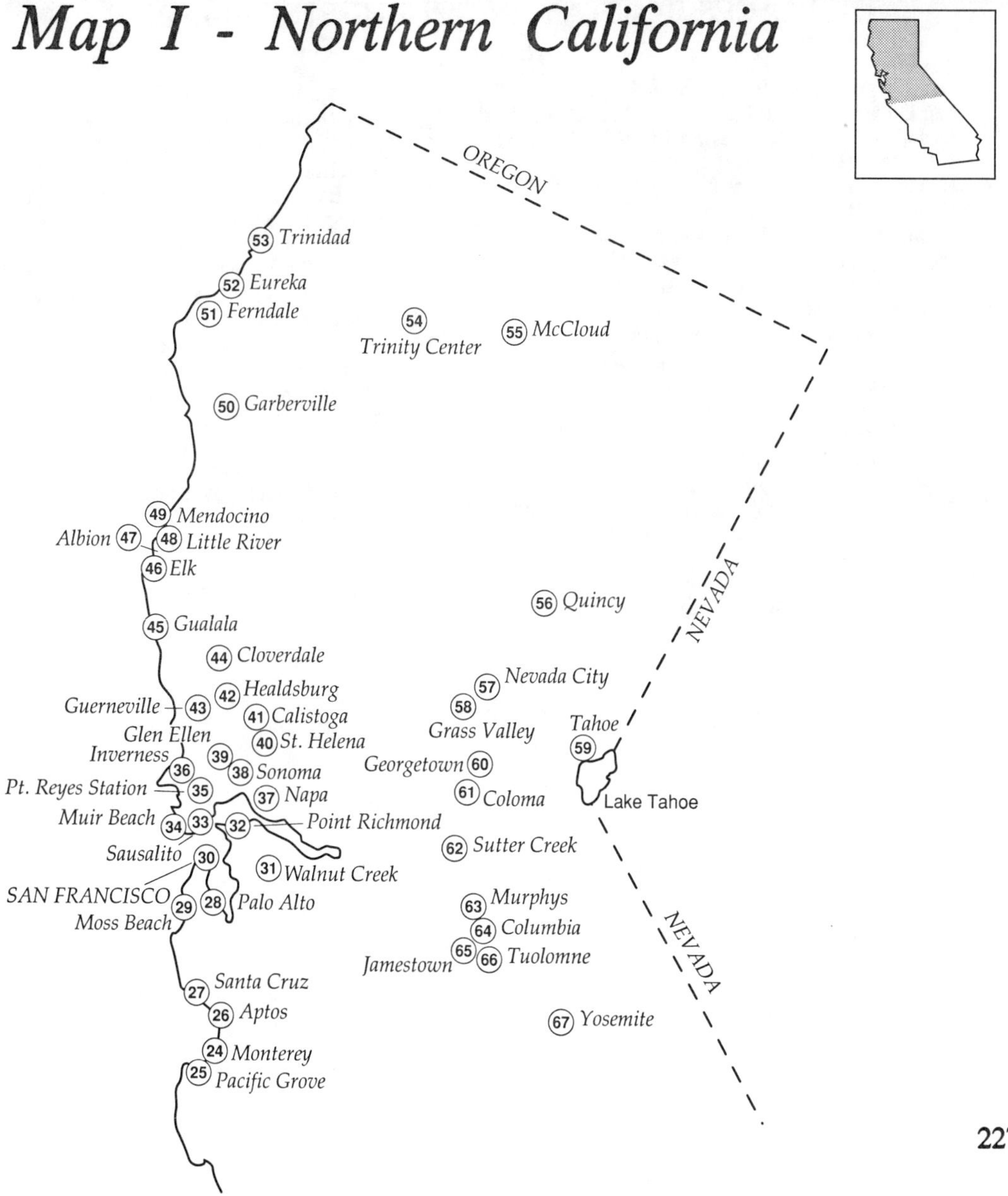

OREGON
53 Trinidad
52 Eureka
51 Ferndale
54 Trinity Center
55 McCloud
50 Garberville
49 Mendocino
Albion 47
48 Little River
46 Elk
56 Quincy
NEVADA
45 Gualala
44 Cloverdale
57 Nevada City
42 Healdsburg
Guerneville 43
41 Calistoga
58 Grass Valley
Tahoe 59
Glen Ellen
40 St. Helena
Inverness
39
36
38 Sonoma
Georgetown 60
Lake Tahoe
Pt. Reyes Station 35
37 Napa
61 Coloma
Muir Beach 34
33
32 Point Richmond
62 Sutter Creek
Sausalito
30
31 Walnut Creek
SAN FRANCISCO
29
28 Palo Alto
63 Murphys
Moss Beach
64 Columbia
NEVADA
Jamestown 65
66 Tuolomne
27 Santa Cruz
26 Aptos
67 Yosemite
24 Monterey
25 Pacific Grove

PLACES TO STAY IN SOUTHERN CALIFORNIA

1 San Diego, Britt House, 36, 189
1 San Diego, Heritage Park Bed & Breakfast, 38, 190
2 La Jolla, The Bed & Breakfast Inn at La Jolla, 39, 152
3 Del Mar, Rock Haus Inn, 128
4 Rancho Santa Fe, Inn at Rancho Santa Fe, 184
5 Dulzura, Brookside Farm B & B Inn, 129
6 Julian, Julian Hotel, 41, 150
7 Idyllwild, Fern Valley Inn, 42, 144
7 Idyllwild, Strawberry Creek Inn, 42, 145
8 Palm Springs, Casa Cody, 177
8 Palm Springs, Ingleside Inn, 178
8 Palm Springs, Villa Royale, 45, 179
9 Big Bear City, Gold Mountain Manor, 106
10 Lake Arrowhead, Eagle's Landing, 153
10 Lake Arrowhead, Saddleback Inn, 47, 154
11 Laguna Beach, Eiler's Inn, 151
12 Newport Beach, Doryman's Inn, 173
13 Avalon - Catalina Island, Garden House Inn, 121
13 Avalon - Catalina Island, Inn on Mt Ada, 122
14 Los Angeles, Salisbury House, 157
14 Los Angeles, Terrace Manor, 158
15 Santa Barbara, The Cheshire Cat, 26, 200
15 Santa Barbara, El Encanto Hotel, 201
15 Santa Barbara, Simpson House Inn, 202
15 Santa Barbara, Tiffany Inn, 203
15 Santa Barbara, The Villa Rosa, 204
15 Santa Barbara - Montecito, San Ysidro Ranch, 205
16 Solvang, El Ranchito, 208
16 Solvang, Tivoli Inn, 209
16 Solvang, Trout Farm, 210
17 Morro Bay, The Inn at Morro Bay, 166
18 Templeton, Country House Inn, 218
19 Cambria, The J. Patrick House, 23, 113
19 Cambria, Olallieberry Inn, 114
20 Coalinga, Inn at Harris Ranch, 124
21 Big Sur, Ventana, 107
22 Carmel Valley, Stonepine, 120
23 Carmel, Cobblestone Inn, 19, 115
23 Carmel, The Happy Landing, 116
23 Carmel, Sea View Inn, 117
23 Carmel, Sundial Lodge, 118
23 Carmel, Vagabond's House Inn, 119
24 Monterey, Old Monterey Inn, 165

Map II - Southern California

24 Monterey
Carmel 23
22 Carmel Valley
21 Big Sur
20 Coalinga
NEVADA
19 Cambria
18 Templeton
17 Morro Bay
16 Solvang
15 Santa Barbara
LOS ANGELES
14
10 Lake Arrowhead
9 Big Bear City
12 Newport Beach
Catalina Island
13 Avalon
11 Laguna Beach
8 Palm Springs
7 Idyllwild
Del Mar 3
4 Rancho Sante Fe
La Jolla 2
6 Julian
San Diego 1
5 Dulzura
MEXICO

Index

INN DISCOVERIES FROM OUR READERS

Future editions of *KAREN BROWN'S COUNTRY INN GUIDES* are going to include a new feature - a list of hotels recommended by our readers. We have received many letters describing wonderful inns you have discovered; however, we have never included them until we had the opportunity to make a personal inspection. This seemed a waste of some marvelous "tips". Therefore, in order to feature them we have decided to add a new section called "Inn Discoveries from Our Readers".

If you have a favorite discovery you would be willing to share with other travellers who love to travel the "inn way", please let us hear from you and include the following information:

1. *Your name, address and telephone number.*

2. *Name, address and telephone number of "your inn".*

3. *Brochure or picture of inn (we cannot return material).*

4. *Written permission to use an edited version of your description.*

5. *Would you want your name, city and state included in the book?*

We are constantly updating and revising all of our guide books. We would appreciate comments on any of your favorites. The types of inns we would love to hear about are those with special old-world ambiance, charm and atmosphere. We need a brochure or picture so that we can select those which most closely follow the mood of our guides. We look forward to hearing from you. Thank you.

Karen Brown's Country Inn Guides

The Most Reliable & Informative Series on Country Inns

Detailed itineraries guide you through the countryside and suggest a cozy inn for each night's stay. In the hotel section, every listing has been inspected and chosen for its romantic ambiance. Charming accommodations reflect every price range, from budget hideaways to deluxe palaces.

Order Form

KAREN BROWN'S COUNTRY INN GUIDES

Please ask in your local bookstore for KAREN BROWN'S COUNTRY INN guides. If the books you want are unavailable, you may order directly from the publisher.

AUSTRIAN COUNTRY INNS & CASTLES $12.95

CALIFORNIA - COUNTRY INNS & ITINERARIES $12.95

ENGLISH, WELSH & SCOTTISH COUNTRY INNS $12.95

EUROPEAN COUNTRY CUISINE - ROMANTIC INNS & RECIPES $10.95

EUROPEAN COUNTRY INNS - BEST ON A BUDGET $14.95

FRANCE - BEST BED & BREAKFASTS $12.95

FRENCH COUNTRY INNS & CHATEAUX $12.95

GERMAN COUNTRY INNS & CASTLES $12.95

IRISH COUNTRY INNS $12.95

ITALIAN COUNTRY INNS & VILLAS $12.95

PORTUGUESE COUNTRY INNS & POUSADAS $12.95

SCANDINAVIAN COUNTRY INNS & MANORS $12.95

SPANISH COUNTRY INNS & PARADORS $12.95

SWISS COUNTRY INNS & CHALETS $12.95

Name ______________________ *Street* ______________________

City ______________________ *State* ______ *Zip* __________

Add $2.50 for the first book and .50 for each additional book for postage & packing.
California residents add 7% sales tax.
Indicate the number of copies of each title. Send in form with your check to:

KAREN BROWN'S COUNTRY INN GUIDES
P.O Box 70
San Mateo, CA 94401
Tel: (415) 342-9117, Fax: (415) 342-9153

This guide is especially written for the individual traveller who wants to plan his own vacation. However, should you prefer to join a group, Town and Country - Hillsdale Travel can recommend tours using country inns with romantic ambiance for many of the nights' accommodation. Or, should you want to organize your own group (art class, gourmet society, bridge club, church group, etc.) and travel with friends, custom tours can be arranged using small hotels with special charm and appeal. For further information please call:

Town & Country - Hillsdale Travel
16 East Third Avenue
San Mateo, California 94401

(415) 342-5591
Outside California 800-227-6733

CLARE BROWN has been a travel consultant since 1969, specializing in planning European countryside itineraries featuring charming small hotels. Now her expertise is available to a much larger audience - the readers of her daughter Karen's Country Inn guides. Clare lives in the San Francisco Bay area with her husband, Bill. Their son, Bill, and his wife, Heidi, live nearby with their three children. Another daughter, Kimberly, is studying hotel management in Colorado.

JUNE BROWN, who was born in Sheffield, England, has an extensive background in travel dating back to her school-girl days when she "youth hosteled" throughout Europe. When June moved to California, she worked as a travel consultant before joining her friend Karen to assist in the research, writing and production of her Country Inn guides. June now lives in the San Francisco Bay area with her husband, Tony, their teen-aged son, Simon, and baby daughter, Clare.

BARBARA TAPP, the talented professional artist who is responsible for most of the interior sketches in *California Country Inns & Itineraries*, always saves time from her busy art and homemaking schedule to help her friend Karen with the illustrations for her Country Inn guides. Born and raised in Sydney, Australia, Barbara now lives in the San Francisco Bay area with her husband, Richard, their two young sons, Jonathan and Alexander, and their baby daughter, Georgia.

CHRISTINA LADAS, who painted the cover for *California Country Inns & Itineraries*, was born and raised in the New York City area where she still resides with her little friend and helper, daughter Erena. The fact that Christina's mother, interior designer Zoe Ladas, recognized and encouraged her daughter's artistic abilities from a pre-school age contributes to her success today as a well-known artist whose wide range of talent leads her into almost every field of art.

Karen Brown (Herbert) was born in Denver, but has spent most of her life in the San Francisco Bay area where she now lives with her husband, Rick, their little girl, Alexandra, and baby son, Richard. Taking a year off from college, Karen travelled to Europe and wrote French Country Inns & Chateaux, the first in what has grown to be an extremely successful series of 14 guide books on charming places to stay. For many years Karen has been planning to open her own country inn. Her dream will soon come to reality - Karen and her husband, Rick, have bought a beautiful piece of property on the coast south of San Francisco and are working with an architect to design the "perfect" little inn which will be furnished with the antiques she has been collecting for many years and will incorporate her wealth of information on just what makes an inn very special. Karen and Rick are looking forward to welcoming guests and friends to their inn.